# HAND-TAMING
# WILD BIRDS
# AT THE FEEDER

# HAND-TAMING WILD BIRDS AT THE FEEDER

BY ALFRED G. MARTIN

*with Photographs and Illustrations by
the Author and with Cover Art and
Illustrations by John Sill*

*Alan C. Hood & Company, Inc.*

CHAMBERSBURG, PENNSYLVANIA

Hand-Taming Wild Birds at the Feeder

Copyright © 1963 by Alfred G. Martin

Cover art and Decorations for
Chapters 4, 5, 7, 9, 10, 11, 13
from BIRD IDENTIFICATION CALENDARS illustrated by
John Sill, copyright © 1985, 1987, 1988, 1990, used
by permission of The Stephen Greene Press, an
imprint of Penguin Books USA, Inc.

Manufactured in the United States of America

**Library of Congress Cataloging-in-Publication Data**

Martin, Alfred G., 1896-1974
Hand-taming wild birds at the feeder / by Alfred G. Martin.
p. cm.
Reprint. Originally published: Freeport, ME : Bond Wheelwright,
1963.
ISBN 0-911469-07-9
1. Birds, Attracting of. 2. Hand-taming wild birds. 3. Birds.
4. Birds—Anecdotes. I. Title.
QL676.5.M3348 1991
639.9'78—dc20                                                90-27113
                                                                CIP

ISBN 0-911469-07-9  Paperback

Published by Alan C. Hood & Company, Inc.
Chambersburg, Pennsylvania

10 9 8 7 6 5 4 3

# CONTENTS

# FOREWORD

Alfred Martin's *Hand-Taming Wild Birds at the Feeder* is a unique perspective on wild birds and how feeding can literally be a hands-on adventure. Martin gained his passion for wild birds while working as a bird-catcher in England. He trapped bullfinches, goldfinches, and other "fine songsters" for England's once-flourishing cage-bird trade. Fortunately, songbirds are now protected throughout most of the Northern Hemisphere, and there is growing recognition that wild birds should be enjoyed outdoors. Yet there is still much to learn about patience and animal behavior from Martin's perceptive writing.

*Hand-Taming Wild Birds at the Feeder* is an entertaining reflection on living with birds in backwoods Maine. For some fifty years, Al Martin lived among his cherished north-woods birds, preferring their company to noisy children and intrusive neightbors. As was often characteristic of his era, he shot backyard hawks (now illegal) and other predators from his kitchen window. Yet this white-bearded Maine woodsman had unbounded compassion for songbirds and devoted years to feeding his favorite chickadees and grosbeaks from his weathered outstretched fingertips. It is obvious from his writings that he was a careful observer, and there are many fascinating accounts of individual bird behaviors.

Martin guides the reader through eleven steps to win the confidence of wild birds. Tips such as "never approaching without speaking" and "never holding out your hand unless it contains food that the bird will like" are useful tips from this seasoned bird enthusiast. The book is packed with Martin's dry humor and backyard experiences in winning the confidence of wild birds.

Al Martin advises that anyone who can stand still for five to ten minutes at a time can lure birds to take food from the hand, but it will take many such encounters to succeed. Black-capped chickadees are usually the first to accept food from the hand, but Martin also provides tips for hand-feeding purple finches, ruby-throated humming-birds, gray catbirds, American robins, and many more.

It's not easy to stand perfectly still with an out-stretched arm for five minutes, especially for those of us who are usually speeding through life. But there is wisdom in the ways of this kind man from Great Pond, Maine. His call for patience and compassion for the individual bird is a refreshing message that there are great rewards close at hand for those who take the time to close the gap between themselves and wild birds.

STEPHEN W. KRESS, PH.D.
Research Biologist
National Audubon Society
Ithaca, New York
February 1991

# HAND-TAMING
# WILD BIRDS
# AT THE FEEDER

# AUTHOR'S NOTE

Dear Reader:

I feel that the best way to begin this book is to apologize to you for the way it is written. In my youth I put considerable time into the study of birds, but very little into the study of correct speech and the written word.

I have tried to write in a way that will be immediately understood by a child of twelve and enjoyed by an adult who is more interested in taming wild birds than in fine journalism. Even a scholar can struggle through it without too much pain, for it will tell him enough about the taming of birds to be worth his while.

Before entering my teens I had already spent considerable time collecting birds for a jobber who lived in the town of Walthamstow, England, where I spent eight years of my childhood. Mr. Buckmaster supplied agents with songbirds for the English pet market.

The wild birds I collected were taken on the outskirts of Epping Forest, along the banks of the River Lea, and in fields, hedgerows, and meadows close by. The greatest demand was for finches, which included the bullfinch, goldfinch, chaffinch, and other fine songsters. Some of the soft-billed birds also had a good market value, especially the song thrush, blackbird, and skylark.

Several other birds were in demand because of their beauty, and these included the greenfinch, hawfinch, yellowhammer, and robin (not like ours but a small red-breasted warbler type. Our robin was known in England as the American red-breasted thrush).

Mr. Buckmaster would never take a nervous bird. He would not buy one until it had lost all fear of man.

1

Some of the trapped birds would never tame; the older they were, the less chance there was of taming them. We always examined them carefully, and if the feet were the least bit rough or the bill scaly, the bird was set free.

If a newly trapped bird did not eat inside of four hours he was released. Most of the younger ones would eat soon after being placed in the small training cage. The sooner a bird fed, the quicker he tamed.

Buckmaster would not take a soft-billed bird that had been trapped; his instructions were to take the song thrush, blackbird, and skylark from the nest just before their eyes opened. This was a rather difficult job. The skylark's nest is extremely hard to find, even more difficult to locate than that of our own meadow lark. The skylark will never leave her nest directly, but will run through the long grass for a hundred feet or more before showing herself. The male always sings a little louder when he is directly over the nest; but even then, in a large field it is still hard to find. Unlike our own larks, the English skylark does all his serenading from the air. He leaves the grass at a slight angle, then goes up and up until he is almost out of sight, and he sings his beautiful song all the time he is in the air. Sometimes he drops rapidly, and when he is about a hundred feet above the nest his song increases in tempo and volume; then up he goes again twinkling like a tiny sparrow hawk in the blue sky.

Sometimes you are lucky and find a nest of larks ready for you to take. If you find a nest with fresh eggs you have to be very careful not to touch it, or the parent birds may desert it. You may find a hatch of babies with their eyes already open, or a nestful of addled eggs (eggs that are well along with babies). You cannot handle these to sun-

2

candle them since the hen will desert the nest if you touch them; you have to guess at the time of incubation.

Occasionally, after spending a lot of time locating a nest and waiting for the babies to hatch, you may find your time has been wasted, when only two birds are produced. I have never known a collector who was callous enough to leave less than two babies for the parents.

Soft-billed baby birds had, of course, to be raised by hand. This would be a time-consuming job if they each required different food, but they all ate hard-boiled egg, pressed through a fine-meshed strainer and mixed with about an equal amount of mashed, boiled potato and a little very finely chopped raw meat. Soft-bill babies did very well on this food, and in less than two weeks were larger than their parents, and soon were able to take care of themselves. They were very tame, had no fear whatever of man, seemed contented in their cages, and would not miss the freedom they had never known.

Collecting the finches was a very simple matter. Once you found the right place to set out the traps, all you had to do was visit them each morning and evening, collect the birds, reset the traps, and put in fresh seed and water.

During the nesting season I roamed the woods and fields, searching for nests of the species I wished to trap later; this way I was able to get many of the young birds soon after nesting was over. These tamed much more easily and took less time than older birds.

The trap cage is a neat little rig with top and bottom sections. The bottom holds a tame male bird of the specie you wish to trap. The upper part holds a small wooden feeder. When a wild bird drops on it to feed, a trap door is sprung.

The tame bird used as a decoy is known as a "caller." Some callers make more money for their owners than others. A good one can hear the note of one of his kind at a great distance. He also has a very loud voice and can instantly call his brother to the trap. But sometimes a caller will sit like a mute and let a large flock of his own kind go by.

Collectors are just as proud of their callers as we are of our prize-winning cats, dogs, or horses. Sometimes they get together in a tavern to talk birds, and after a few ales, the bragging starts. Some of the collectors even come to blows protecting the reputation of their respective callers.

Caller contests are sometimes scheduled on a nice Sunday, and collectors come from miles around. Only one bird is allowed for each contestant. Bets are placed, and occasionally one caller is put up against another as ante instead of cash. The best bird does not always win. A beautiful cock chaffinch who had been champ for three years was disqualified because a bird of another specie — a female greenfinch — dropped into the trap cage.

I was very lucky in trapping greenfinches. My call bird "Greenie" had been raised in captivity and was quite tame. He always took his daily bath in a soup dish on the table in my room. One morning as he was about to hop into the dish, he suddenly stood bolt upright, let out a loud call note, and flew to the window. He called twice and in a few seconds three wild greenfinches were peeking through the pane at him. I immediately put Greenie in a trap cage, hung it on the side of the house near the window, and set up five more traps above it. A little later I sat at the table eating my English breakfast of soft-roed bloater while Greenie called, and soon I could hear the little trap doors falling. Before I had finished breakfast I had five new greenfinches, including one beautiful cock that was pure white except for a bright yellow bar on the edge of each wing.

I hand-fed my first wild bird, a female hedge sparrow, at the age of ten. Many years later, on a year's stay in England, I spent most of my time sketching the beautiful scenery of Epping Forest and getting friendly with the wild birds. I always carried raisins in one pocket and canary seed in another. I was successful in hand-feeding the blackbird with raisins and the chaffinch and bullfinch with seed. While sketching, I would listen for bird notes and when I noticed a bird feeding on the ground, I would very cautiously get as close as I could and let seed or raisins slip gently through my fingers. Sometimes the bird would leave and not return. Sometimes he would return, and find me lying motionless, with my arm extended and fingers flat on the ground with seed on my palm. It usually took all day and sometimes longer before a bird would approach my hand; and very few did.

But I am certain that the methods of hand-taming wild birds given in this book would be just as successful with British birds. The song thrush and blackbird can be finger-tamed with raisins and cooking currants; the titmouse would take sunflower seed; and the finches would take any mixture of seed that contains thistle and flax.

When we moved to Massachusetts I set up a fair-sized aviary and soon had a good variety of foreign finches, siskins, buntings, and canaries. I spent a lot of money on it but had a lot of fun, and raised some nice crosses, mules, and hybrids. Like hundreds of bird lovers around the globe, I wanted to be the first to raise a red canary. When you see a very deep orange or red-colored canary you can be pretty certain that one of his ancestors was either a male African fire finch or Venezuelan hooded red siskin. The closest I ever came to a red canary was a beautiful, slender, second-cross male from a rose finch—Mexican red-headed linnet hybrid and a buff Yorkshire canary female. He was a solid cardinal red, but his wings were a muddy brown.

Of all the pleasure I have had with birds, none has given me as much as the wild ones that feed from my lips and hands here at Great Pond, Maine.

# 1

All you need to be successful in taming wild birds is a little know-how. You have most likely heard someone say: "She has wonderful luck with her flowers." Luck plays a very small part in success with flowers — no more than it does with birds.

Here are a few simple but very important rules you must remember if you wish to succeed with birds:

1. Whether you believe it or not, always try to behave as if a bird can and does reason, as if in some things he is smarter than you. If you do this, you will have little trouble in hand-taming him.

2. Never approach a wild bird without speaking to it all the time.

3. Always move very slowly around birds until they become accustomed to your presence.

4. Always try to remember that there is no such thing as a naturally tame wild bird. You are his greatest enemy until you have gained his confidence. If you should have a stray one come to your hand before you have tried to hand-tame him, you can be sure that he has been tamed by some other bird lover.

5. Never hold out your hand to a bird unless it contains food that he likes. A wild bird does not come to you because he loves you, he takes a chance because he is hungry. Holding out

an empty hand to a bird is like holding out an empty hand to a child who expects to find a candy bar in it. A bird will resent it as much as a child would, and worse still, he may think you are telling him that the food is all gone, and he may leave for greener pastures.

6.   Always carry some of the seed you are feeding in your pocket, then if a bird settles on your shoulder he will not be disappointed.

7.   Never swallow while a bird is on your hand watching you. This rule is a result of consistent experience on my part. Until I realized what was wrong, I lost the opportunity to tame many birds. The sight of food makes a bird's mouth water, and he always swallows just before he starts to eat. When he sees you swallow while you are looking at him, he may think you are considering him for your next meal. He won't stay around to find out; the chances are very good that you will never see that bird again.

Always watch for the slightest sign of fear on a bird's face. His eyes show fear in exactly the same way human eyes do. The movement of a bird's stomach also shows fear, just as the rapid movement of the vein on a man's forehead betrays his fear.

The instant you see signs of fear, when a wild bird first comes to  your hand, hold your breath as long as you  can and keep absolutely motionless.

There are a great many little things like this that are hard to explain, but if you are very observant they will come to you with experience.

A great many bird lovers who have tamed birds to eat from their hand have found that they cannot get good movie films of them because they will not stay long enough. The reason for this is simply that the tamer fails to notice that the birds are frightened by the camera.

If you are taking movies of a wild bird you must realize that the noise of the camera sounds like a truck to his sensitive ears, and the instant you see him show fear, you must stop the camera and wait. If the bird stays, you can start taking pictures again.

I have a few friends who come here with their cameras because they have not been able to get pictures of their own birds.

A friend from Massachusetts came to get some hummingbird movies. I sat him near my feeder and placed a syrup cup in his hand, and told him to move the cup very slowly toward his face and to watch for my stop and go signals.

A hummingbird soon came to the cup, took a drink, then backed up. The cup was moving very slowly; the bird started toward it but hovered — *Stop,* I signaled. The cup stopped and the bird took another drink — *Start,* the cup moved and the bird followed and hovered again — *Stop,* the bird drank again. Each time I ordered *Stop,* I stopped my friend's camera. After three signals, the bird went into the cup without hesitation, and I kept the camera rolling for two more drinks while the cup was held four inches in front of my friend's nose. When we finished we had a four-foot run of film.

8. Never close your hand on a wild bird unless it is to pick up a sick or injured one. The instant you close your hand on a free bird, he is

**9**

so frightened that when you open your hand again, he will fly as far away from you as he can and will not return. Some birds of the same specie are more timid than others. On more than one occasion I have heard and felt the tiny heart of a poor little bird burst from fright while I held him in my hand.

9.    If a bird wants to leave you while you are trying to tame him, let him go, do not follow him. He knows how the fox, mink, weasel, cat, and raccoon follow a bird when they want something to eat, and when you start following him, he thinks you have the same thing in mind. Be patient and the bird will come to you when he is hungry.

10.    Never overload your feeder, unless you are trying to get a large flock of new birds to come in. If you have plenty of food out all the time, you will encourage undesirable species, and you will fail in hand-taming a single bird. It is impossible to hand-tame a wild bird that can get all the food he wants on your feeder; he must be hungry before he will take a chance on your hand.

11.    Never allow even your best friends near your birds unless you are with them. A well-meaning friend can ruin months of work for you and may even drive your birds off for good. If you wish to let a friend feed your birds, be very sure to advise him how to do it first, and if he will not do exactly as told, get him away as fast as you can, or you may be very sorry.

When it becomes known that you have hand-tamed birds you will have a lot of visitors. You will be expected to drop everything and give your company your whole attention. Sometimes a group of visitors who have taken up an hour of your time will leave as a new group arrives. You may find that you cannot eat your lunch if you wish to be polite. I have seen many days when company has kept me from work that was very important to me. It is impossible to go through a season without hurting someone's feelings, so I finally decided, a long time ago, to toss what good manners I had and think of myself for a change.

Your understanding of wild creatures is something that the average person cannot grasp because he cannot see the little things that are so obvious to you; he has never studied birds as you have, and naturally will be offended if you refuse to let him near yours. His feelings will be hurt if you appear to give more consideration to an animal than you do to his entertainment.

I recall an incident that took place four years back: Mr. and Mrs. X had visited my studio for several years; they were fine photographers and made many beautiful pictures here at my place, and I enjoyed their visits. One day they brought a friend, and I asked them to show him around, for Mrs. X had found a baby deer mouse that had fallen out of its nest in my yard and I wanted to study it. "The mouse comes first," I said. The three of them walked out, and I have not seen them since! They did not know that I was interested in white-footed mice and wanted to find out whether a mother white-foot would adopt a strange baby and care for it.

You will very likely have visitors with children who want to chase and catch your birds. The parents will most likely say: "Isn't that cute!" or "Please, dear, don't frighten the birds," but they stand there and do nothing

**11**

about it. If this happens at your feeder, there are two things you can do; you can keep quiet and watch weeks of tiresome work ruined, or you can forget your manners and kick them all out . . . I now have no manners at all, but I *do* have birds.

Incidentally, you may want to know what I found out about the deer mouse. At this time I had a pair in a large aquarium; they had built their nest and were feeding three half-grown babies. As soon as my friends left, I placed the baby on the floor of the aquarium and sat down to see what would happen. I did not have to wait more than a minute. The mother came out of her nest and went right over to the baby; she sniffed it a few times, then went back. I could see some action in the nest; the top part of it was being pushed up an inch or two. In a few seconds she came out again, took the baby by the scruff of its neck, and carried it up and into her nest.

The following morning I gently moved the piece of bark that formed one side of the nest foundation and found that the mother had built a neat little nest on the roof of the first one, and the adopted baby was curled up inside. I had lost two friends, but I did learn that a little white-footed mouse will adopt a strange baby even though she has her own family to care for.

You will have greater success with birds if you think of them as little people who can reason, and not as brainless creatures who act only on the persuasion of some inborn instinct.

Two years ago last winter, an officer and his wife from Dow Air Force Base visited my studio to see the mounted specimens and paintings. He was very much interested in my paintings, all of which are of fish, birds, and

12

animals with natural backgrounds. I noticed he was picking out the best ones for a closer look. He turned to me and was about to speak when a pine grosbeak called for a hand-out. The airman's wife turned sharply and asked:

"Who is that?"

I instantly knew she was a bird lover.

"That is Mr. Pine Grosbeak," I replied.

"May I please see him? I've never had the pleasure."

"That's a new one on me, too," the officer said.

I asked them to follow me, while I took six sun-flower seeds from my pocket and handed them to the lady. I let her go first. She very slowly opened the kitchen door and stood in the doorway holding out the seeds for the bird, who immediately settled on her hand to feed. She spoke softly to him:

"Hello, sweetheart, my what a handsome little fellow you are!"

He was a fine old cock with a deep orange coloring. After he had polished off the six seeds, he looked up and asked for more.

"Not now," the lady said, "later on. You little ones are all alike; you'd eat a body out of house and home."

The bird may not have understood her words as we would, but he knew exactly what she meant and flew to a nearby apple tree to eat buds.

I have known many good naturalists in my time, but I think my friend Father Daniel O'Keefe of St. Mary's Church in Holliston, Massachusetts, has more bird know-how than any of them.

I have seen him walk up to within three feet of a wild bird and talk to it while the bird stayed right there and listened as if he understood every word. Perhaps he did. Who knows?

I once found a day-old purple finch on the ground under a ruined nest that hung in a fir tree. The tiny chick was no bigger than a bumble bee. She was cold, and showed little signs of life. I closed my hand around her and soon the warmth revived her a little. I took her home with me and made her a nest of deer hair and cotton which I put down on top of a small light bulb, for warmth, in a strawberry box. Two artificial canary eggs were placed in with the baby to give her support. Without them she could very easily mature with crippled legs. I then mixed a little pablum with water and gave her her first meal.

With my mother's help I raised this finch to be the tamest cage bird I have ever known.

My mother had named her "Cindy." Later, when I told Father Dan about Cindy, he wanted to see her right away. I told him to go easy because Cindy was afraid of strangers. My mother sat at the kitchen table, I stood in the center of the large room, and Father Dan stood behind me and a few feet to my right. Cindy had the freedom of the kitchen and now sat on the edge of the open doorframe of her cage. I called her and she came right out, but instead of settling on my outstretched hand as she usually did, she went right past me and settled on the lapel of Father Dan's jacket; then she climbed up to his collar and nibbled gently on the lobe of his ear. She looked around at his face and chirped a few very sweet notes to him.

Most of my ornithologist friends would ask: "How are all your birds, Al?"

Father O'Keefe would say: "How are all the little folk getting along?"

**14**

# 2

There are many types of feeders on the market today, and most of them will answer the purpose, but I have found that wild birds come more readily to one that is made of some natural-looking material; I think my style of feeders will give you better results.

On my kitchen window sill I have a slab of wood with the bark left on. This is cut a little shorter than the sill to allow for expansion in wet weather. A finish nail in the middle and two on each end anchor the slab to the sill. (These finish nails should be driven in flush to the bark, otherwise a bird may leave one of his eyes on the nailhead while picking up seed.) The recesses in the rough bark keep the wind from blowing all the seed away.

Close to the outside of my kitchen door, I have a twelve-foot balsam fir tree. On the south side of this tree and about shoulder-high, I trimmed out a few branches back to the trunk, to form a sort of cave about two feet square. Copper wire woven closely across the lower branches of this cave make a foundation to hold a piece of turf with soil and grass attached. This encourages visits from birds such as juncos, towhees, and sparrows who otherwise would stay on the ground; it also makes a nice rest for a tired arm while taming the birds.

Close to the fir tree and about six feet above the doorstep, I hung a piece of dead pine on the wall. It is in its natural log shape, about ten inches in diameter and two and a half feet long. There is a natural woodpecker's hole near the top that cuts in about three inches. Every morning I press a walnut-sized piece of suet back in the hole, out of sight of jays. If a large amount of suet is used, the jays soon spot it and carry it off before a woodpecker or nuthatch can get to it. For the chickadees, I melt the suet and pour some into small holes on the feeder log or into the bark crevices, where it hardens and is also safe from jays.

If I expect camera company, I take a pan of melted suet out to the fir tree, bend some of the lower branches down, and dip the tips into the liquid. As soon as the suet sets, I let it spring back into its natural position. Redpolls and chickadees will cling upside-down and pick off the tiny pieces of suet, and this makes beautiful movies at close range.

Most people who maintain small feeders use the packaged wild bird seed now sold all over the states. This seed is very inexpensive, and I use a lot of it myself. If you are using it, you have probably noticed that some of it is not eaten. Here at my feeders, finches and grosbeaks will not touch the kafir corn. But if mourning doves should happen along they would take the corn first. The seed companies are well aware of this selectivity and do their best to give you a mixture that is not too expensive and yet will contain some food for all types of grain eaters.

For winter feeding in Maine the ordinary packaged wild bird seed does very well, but for the year-round, for a greater variety of birds, I have found that a few extra seeds added to the mixture give better results. Purple finches, pine siskins, and goldfinches will stay longer at my feeders if I add a pound each of flax, rape, and niger.

If you maintain large feeders and can afford the very best for your birds, you might try one of the special mixtures that are used in large aviaries and by cage-bird breeders throughout the world. These are expensive because they contain seeds imported from many foreign countries,

**16**

including Holland, Spain, Africa, Turkey, France, and India. For a hundred-pound bag, f.o.b. New York, Psyllium seed costs twenty-five dollars; Teazle costs thirty-five dollars; Gold of Pleasure, forty; Grains of Paradise, fifty; and Saffron, ninety dollars. The "vitamin mixtures" are very good and not too expensive. These go under several trade names, but they all contain about the same mixture of seeds, which are always as fresh as the market season allows. Most of them — with the exception of hemp seed, which is sterilized by our Narcotics Bureau — will germinate in your garden.

"Surelife" is the brand I use, and it has kept my birds in tiptop condition. In the spring of 1961, "Surelife Vitamin Mix" cost about fourteen dollars a hundred-pound bag, f.o.b. New York (The Hershey Company, 189 Washington Street). I used it for community breeding, allowing a number of males and females to mate at random in a large enclosure. To one hundred pounds of Surelife I added five pounds of "Special Goldfinch Mix," and this with the necessary fruit and greens, kept the following birds in top condition: a dozen female canaries, a male African fire finch, an Australian fire finch, a Mexican rainbow bunting, a Venezuelan red siskin, a Russian goldfinch, a Mexican red-headed linnet, and an English rose linnet. I figure on about a soupspoon a day of seed per bird.

Most of these birds, especially the siskin and goldfinches, seemed to prefer the niger seed. Niger is a native of Africa and a member of the thistle family. I once planted some of the seed I picked out of Surelife, and when it was ripe the plants were full of goldfinches. The blooms did not resemble the spiny thistle as I know it, but looked just like miniature sunflowers in bush form. The flowers were yellow, about an inch across, and grew in clusters. It was not until the seeds had ripened that I was sure I had not planted

**17**

the wrong kind. The little Venezuelan siskin seemed to live almost entirely on niger.

Canaries found all the seed they wanted in Sure-life, and the wild-trapped foreign finches found plenty of their natural food; it made no difference if the finch came from Mexico, England, or Africa, he found what he wanted.

If you wish to keep robins, catbirds, and thrushes at your feeder, you can put out cooking currants and seedless raisins (the dark-colored ones are the best to use). A crushed apple is appreciated by these birds, and grosbeaks like it too.

There are a great many so-called "treats" on the market today that may be harmful to your birds. A lot of them will make a bird sing, but may kill him if he gets enough. Some of these are nothing but crushed hemp and poppy seed mixed with syrup to form a biscuit or toy-like ornament.

I once killed a valuable pair of birds by feeding them some. Treats are all right if used very sparingly, but zoos and aviaries never use them.

Peanut butter and avocados are fine for us, but can also be very harmful to birds. I once killed a very fine bird by giving him a piece of avocado because he asked for it.

Squirrels fed on raw peanuts keep in fine condition, but cooked peanuts will make them bloaty and sluggish, and their fur loses its gloss. I am very fond of peanut butter and eat a lot of it, but I never give it to my birds. Some people live on one type of food, others on something quite different. Some chickadees and redpolls will eat only a very little peanut butter; others will eat a lot, and a few will eat nothing else as long as the butter is available.

When a seed-eating bird feeds entirely on peanut butter, he loses the gravel from his gizzard, and it does not function normally; it shrinks and his liver becomes enlarged, and the bird is soon very ill or dead.

Some chickadees die soon after eating their first meal of peanut butter. When they have eaten all they can hold, they cram their little mouths full of it and carry it away. When they try to deposit the butter in a hiding place, it sticks to the roof of their mouths; in the struggle to dislodge it, the butter is packed tighter and the birds choke to death.

If a female chickadee eats a lot of peanut butter up to the time she is ready to lay her first egg, she is very apt to die of egg-binding. Some of my naturalist friends disagree with me on this, but I have had several chickadees left at my taxidermy studio that had died this way, and every one of them had been eating peanut butter.

The following incident took place in 1944.

As I was leaving the Public Library one morning in the beautiful town of Norwood, Massachusetts, I noticed two little girls on the front lawn who were looking down at a small moving object. It was a chickadee trying to get off the ground. I picked up the bird and knew instantly that she was egg-bound. I told the children I would take her home with me and make her well, then bring her right back.

I called a taxi over and was home in a few minutes. I heated some water to the boiling point, placed a towel over the steaming pan, and held the bird over the moist heat. She soon dropped her egg on the towel, and the scent of peanut butter rose with the steam.

I was not greatly surprised to find the little girls waiting for me at the library. Both ran to meet me, and one of them said: "Did you?"

For answer I took the chickadee from my pocket, and her bright eyes blinked as she looked at them. I opened

**19**

my hand and the bird lay still for a few seconds, then stood on my thumb while she looked around a bit. She preened her feathers under one wing, then the other, and shook herself all over; she preened under her tail, said "peep," then bounced through the air to a fir tree across the street on the Plimpton estate.

If it had not been for my experience in the aviary, I would not have known that the chickadee was egg-bound, or how to handle her, and she would have died.

Many bird lovers will not agree with me on the peanut butter question, and I see no reason why they should, as long as their chickadees appear to be healthy and enjoy the butter they are given. But I hope they never have to watch a tiny chickadee choke to death or die from eggbinding or other ailments caused by peanut butter!

Some birds will feed almost entirely at the feeder and will try any kind of food they find on or near it.

A few years ago I made the mistake of throwing some table scraps on the deep snow in my yard. At this time a large flock of purple finches, three slate juncos, and a cowbird were steady boarders at the feeder. When I threw out the scraps, the cowbird began picking at a piece of fried haddock. He ate nothing else that day and the next morning. Just before dusk on the second day he sat all puffed up beside the piece of fish. I put him in the casualty cage. The next morning he was dead. The fish had not spoiled in the zero weather, so the cowbird had not been poisoned, but for some reason a full diet of cooked fish had killed him.

Birds of prey are sometimes a problem at the feeder, especially in rural sections. Some people allow a predator to help himself to their tame birds because they feel they would be interfering with "Nature's great scheme" if they destroyed the predator. These people are usually "book naturalists" who have had little or no experience with Nature.

The feeder is not a part of "Nature's scheme," it is built by man and stocked with unseasonable food, and has little to do with Nature. The person who maintains a bird feeder is responsible for any deaths due to predators; he has assembled the birds at his feeder; he has tolled in the predator with those birds, and it is his duty to protect them, for they have put their trust in him. It is his duty to see that a flock of jays will not rob the smaller birds of the food he puts out for them.

Most predators are now protected by state and federal laws. They should be protected, but the laws should also make allowance for the protection of birds at the feeder. Birds of prey as a whole make little difference in the song-bird population; it is the individual predator who will locate a well-populated feeder and hang around until the last songster is gone. He is the one that should be destroyed. When a bird of prey invades a state or federal fish hatchery or game farm, he is promptly shot. The game farms cannot afford to feed hawks and herons on trout and pheasants that cost from fifty cents to two dollars each to raise. Neither can you afford to feed a hawk on your tame birds that have cost you as much by the time you have them tamed. When I see a bird of prey near my feeder, I watch him carefully; if he takes one bird and does not return for more he is safe; if he returns, I call the game warden.

If you are bothered by a predator you can call your local game warden. He may choose to destroy the predator or he may have some useful ideas to help you protect your tamed birds.

Tame chipmunks are a nuisance because they steal so much food. They go over the feeder like a vacuum cleaner and never miss a seed; but the children love them. If you ever see the expression on a child's face when a chipmunk on his hand stops eating to scratch a flea, you will forget all the chipmunk's bad habits.

They are very entertaining at the feeder if you do not have too many. The method of hand-taming one of them is the same as with birds, and sunflower seed or pie crust is the best food to use. Chipmunks are much easier to tame than the tamest of wild birds.

Chipmunks do not bother birds very much. Occasionally an individual will require a little more fresh meat than others and will take a bird if he gets the chance. All chipmunks will take eggs from the nests, but I never interfere with this unless I have a special reason. I believe the little animals cannot get along without eggs.

A pair of robins had their nest in an apple tree near the house. It was in plain view and eight feet from the ground; it contained four eggs. One day I stood looking up at the nest and was about to climb up to see if another egg had been added to the clutch, when a chipmunk poked his head up from it and peered down at me. All I could see was a blue egg, one eye, and an ear. The chipmunk stood up on the edge of the nest, and the cock robin came at him with terrific speed and knocked him clean off and out about ten feet. He went sailing through the air and smacked on the ground. He didn't land on his feet either; he landed hard on his rear end. How he could take a blow like that and live, I couldn't figure out, but when he went right back up to the nest again, with both robins now diving at him, and got another egg, I was amazed.

22

The only time I butted in on egg-stealing was when I was trying to film the incubation of a nest of red-eyed vireo eggs. I saw a chipmunk take one egg and trapped him and let him go several miles away. An hour later, I was sorry because when I went to see if an egg had hatched, the nest was empty; another chipmunk had already taken the rest of them.

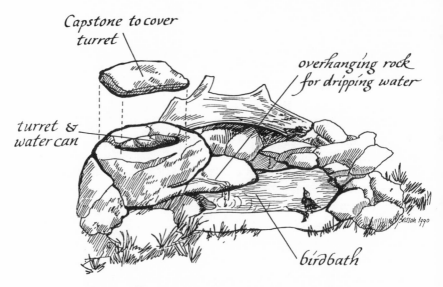

Capstone to cover turret

overhanging rock for dripping water

turret & water can

birdbath

FIG. 1.   Showing open turret or water-can container.

FIG. 2.   Showing finished bath-drinker in operation.   To clean, simply take out water can, sweep out water with a whisk broom, and let the sun dry out the basin for half an hour.

24

# 3

The pictures opposite show the bird bath and fountain I use. I have found that this type of bath is accepted more readily than the pedestal type with a water container on top. The ground birds especially are more apt to use it. And apparently the slow drip of water is seen by birds that would otherwise keep going without noticing the bath.

This type of bath can be built to look just like a natural spring trickling through the rocks. It can also be used as the centerpiece of a beautiful rock garden or as a lily pond and fish pool, depending on the size you make it.

The bath pictured here is a good size for the average front lawn and will take care of a large flock of birds. I would not advise anything smaller than two by three feet, or regardless of shape, six square feet.

All you need to build a bath like the one shown here is five dollars worth of ready-mix cement, some flat rocks, a round can to hold a gallon of water, four or five strips of white pine or other soft wood (the ones I used were one-eighth of an inch thick, one and a half inches wide, and four feet long), several sharpened stakes about a foot high, a foot-long heavy, straight piece of wire, some grease, a few large sheets of fairly tough wrapping paper and some waxed paper, something to mix the cement in, and of course, some water. You are now ready to go to work.

The first thing to do is to choose the site for the bath. This should be on the south or west side of the house if possible. Try to choose a spot that can be watched from a window. Decide what shape you wish the bath to be. It can be anything but square: birds do not like corners. The best shape for a natural effect is an irregular oval. When you have decided on the shape and size, cut away the turf to the measure you wish, then make it a foot larger all around; this will give you a border on which to lay a rock wall. If you lay rocks down on top of grass you will be kept busy clipping, for it will keep growing over into the bath.

Now with the turf cut away, you scoop out the soil to the required depth, leaving the foot-wide border as is. The depression you are forming should be about six inches deep along the middle and a little toward the back. This should be the deepest part; it should rise gradually to the sides until it levels off with the inside edge of the border.

When you have the depression about where you want it, step in it and gently tamp the soil down smooth.

Now make sure you have all the flat rocks you will need and everything else ready for the job. The strips of wood must be thoroughly soaked in water so that they will bend without breaking. A good way to do this is to weight them down in a foot of water in your bathtub. If very hot water is used, they will soften up in a couple of hours. It will take twice as long in cold water.

Soak the sheets of wrapping paper for about an hour, then crumple them up in your hands, being sure not to tear them. When the paper is softened up like a piece of cloth, press it into the depression until it fits close and even on the earth. Sprinkle the paper generously with water to keep it wet while you mix about twenty pounds of the ready-mix cement. Dump this into the center of the depression and smooth it out, working from the middle, until you have a thickness of about an inch; this will keep the paper anchored.

Moisten the paper again, then with a pair of shears trim it around the inside edge of the foot-wide border. Now

26

drive the stakes in around the paper to form a fence that will follow the sides and back only of the shape your bath will be. Bend the wood strips around the stakes to form a solid fence, overlapping them a few inches and driving a stake on the other side of each overlap to hold the strips firmly in place. Now, gently tap the strips down until the bottom edge of the fence rests firmly on the earth, but is not driven into it. It must be close enough to the earth so that wet cement will not leak beneath it.

This operation should go right along without too much delay because the strips of wood must not be allowed to dry out. Mix up some more cement for the space between the fence and the anchoring patch you already have laid. Be sure that the entire depression is covered; spread the cement as evenly as you can in a gentle rise up to one-half inch from the top of the wood strips. Mix more cement to cover the sides and back of the one-foot border, which should be kept flat and even and flush to the outside of the wood strips. Now cement in the front of the border and round it off a little, leveling it off with the natural lawn. Scoop out, or flatten down, the border at the front center, just enough to allow water to flow over when the bath is overloaded.

You now have your bath laid in and are ready for the rock work. On one end of the border, a few inches from the fence, build up a rock and cement foundation about six inches high, keeping it flat and even on the top. Then press a thin flat rock into the still wet cement in position so that part of it overhangs the basin you have made and slopes just enough for water to slowly follow it down and *drip*, not trickle, into the bath. It is the action of the water dripping directly on the surface of the bath that really attracts the birds.

When you have the overhanging rock set in place, thoroughly grease the piece of heavy wire and lay it down the center so that it will extend a few inches beyond the overhang and also back a few inches on the fountain. Hold the wire down firmly while you drop a handful of cement on it, and press a rock down on the cement. This will be the first stone in the turret you are going to build next, within which your water container will be hidden. As soon as the cement is set you can pull the wire out. Now plug the inside hole with a wooden match and make sure as you cement along that the match is not covered.

Smooth off the foundation so that the gallon can (or any size can you want) will set on it without tilting. Be sure to allow plenty of room as you build the turret wall around the can. I find that I have to use a new one every so often, for they rust out. As you cement your rocks in the wall, be sure to keep them tight also, because if any space is left between, dust will get in and clog up the tiny opening you have made with the wire from which the water is to escape.

When your wall is high enough to hide the can, you can top it with an inch of cement. Then, before it sets, cover it with waxed paper and put in the flat rock you will use as a cover for the turret, so the can won't show. Press this down gently until it is embedded about an eighth of an inch in the soft cement, and leave it to set.

The only cementing you have to do now is to set in the rocks around the rest of the border. Be sure to leave a few inches free and clear all around the outside of the wooden fence. When the cement is good and hard and the wood strips dry, they will shrink and can easily be lifted out; the stakes can be pulled up, and you will have a basin with an expansion belt around part of it. It can be taken up or left out all winter and will not crack. Now, pull out the waxed paper. You should find that the top stone will set into its own depression and be tight enough to keep out any foreign matter. You can also take the matchstick plug from the water hole.

The amount of water flow you have will depend upon the size of the hole in the container you use. A tiny slit no bigger than the thickness of a piece of cotton cloth will let out enough water, but a small hole like this very soon gets caked with rust and plugs up. I use a lath nail driven into the can a quarter-inch from the bottom to form the hole, then reversed so that the head of the nail is inside the can; this prevents the flow of water from washing out the nail. There is just enough space around it to allow a slow leak which amounts to about a single drop every second.

If you desire a heavier fall of water you can take out the can and fill up the turret, but of course the water will not run for very long. This makes nice movies when birds are drinking or washing in the bath.

If you have running water and don't mind the expense, you could run a pipe under the lawn and up into the turret. Put a tap on the pipe, then you can regulate it to any size flow you wish, and it could be turned off every evening.

When you are satisfied with the water flow, the only thing left to do is to place flat rocks over the space left around the basin for expansion. Be sure it is completely covered, otherwise a bird may get his feet caught in it and break a leg.

You could of course, have all this work done for you and perhaps get a nicer job than my set-up, but it is a lot of fun doing it yourself.

If your bath is in the open, it would be wise to plant a few thick shrubs or small evergreens close to it. A wet bird is easy prey for a predator unless he has a place to hide and can get there fast.

**4**

Almost any person who can sit or stand still for five or ten minutes at a time can hand-tame a wild bird at the feeder. But it takes many more than one five or ten minutes to complete the job!

Here at Great Pond, chickadees spend more time at the feeder than other birds, and I have found them the easiest to tame.

**BLACK-CAPPED CHICKADEE**

Wait until these have been coming to your feeder for about a week, then take all the seed and suet away. An hour later, place a few sunflower seeds at a spot where you can comfortably rest your hand. Place a few more as far away from where your hand will rest as the size of your feeder will allow. Watch and listen for a chickadee, and as soon as you see or hear one, go out to the feeder and get as comfortable as you can with your hand in position. The bird may not come right away — this is where your patience comes in — but when it does come close, you must stand perfectly still and not move your hand. The eyes of a bird are very sharp and he has already taken in the situation. If you get too tired or tense, go into the house and rest a while, then take up again where you left off.

The bird will finally come to the feeder while your hand rests on it. He may scold you a little or buzz around a bit; but remain very still. After he has taken a few seeds from the farther side of the feeder, move the remaining ones a little closer to where your hand will rest. When the

31

chickadee is taking seed no more than a foot from your hand you should call it quits for the day.

Early the next morning, make sure there is no food on the feeder, but place a few seeds at the spot where the bird came closest to your hand. Now hold your hand flat on the feeder, palm up, with a few seeds on it. Get comfortable, and wait. This is the time to be very careful. Speak to the bird softly when he comes, but do not move or turn your head to look at him; if your throat tickles, do not swallow. If you must do something about it, try coughing gently.

By now the chickadee should have taken the seed from the feeder and when he returns for more, the only seed available is on your hand; he must get it there or go without; he always gets it.

Usually, when a wild bird first feels the strange texture of your fingers, he lets go immediately. If this happens, keep talking to him gently and do not move a finger. After a little while, since he is very hungry for that seed, he will again settle on your hand. This time he will stay.

Take your time, do not rush him or you will never tame him. When a chickadee has been feeding on your hand about a dozen times without fear, you can start moving your hand. Do it very slowly and smoothly, watching him carefully for the least sign of nervousness. Watch his stomach: the instant you see it throb, stop your hand movement. If you do not, the bird will leave and may not return. As he becomes accustomed to your slight movements, you can increase them gradually. After a while, you can walk around at normal gait with the bird on your hand. He will also fly to you and feed while you walk.

Chickadees become very tame once you have their

**32**

confidence; they are wonderfully entertaining, and your friends will love them.

My good friend the Reverend Ron A. Mosley and I were taking a short cut through a thick stand of young balsam fir trees on my wood lot in the winter of 1959 when he asked me if I would sell him about fifty trees. I told him he could have them for nothing if he did the work himself. A few weeks later, Ron arrived with a group of his young people who were members of the Senior High Pilgrim Fellowship. It would be their job to harvest and sell the Christmas trees as part of a benefit program for the Bar Harbor Congregational Church.

I picked up my movie camera and went into the woods with the group. We got a good fire going on the snow, hung a large kettle of cocoa over it, and put a gallon of lemonade on the snow for the more rugged workers. In a few minutes the axes were ringing. At the first sound, a deer bounded out of the thicket and gave a good show as she went up over a blowdown and disappeared.

A few hours later the group were sitting around the fire eating sandwiches and drinking steaming hot cocoa or almost frozen lemonade. I had taken movies of the tree cutting and of the group eating lunch afterward. Now I wanted to get a few birds into the film. A pretty girl and two of the older boys had stopped in a small clearing to examine some firs; the sun was shining right down on them and the background of pines and firs was ideal. I gave each a few sunflower seeds with the instruction to stand very still while offering the food.

I called for at least five minutes, but no birds came or answered. The young people lost interest and were about to give up when I heard a chickadee about two hun-

dred yards away. I called again and immediately got a..
answer. Another call, and in a few seconds the bird settled
on my hand. I introduced him to my new friends and
stepped back, and the chickadee flew off with a sunflower
seed and was back again in a few seconds with his whole
family. Back and forth they went until the last seed was
gone. The young people got a tremendous thrill out of it.
They could hardly believe that these wild birds had been
called to them from so far away and had taken food from
their hands.

**5**

I have found the nuthatch a difficult bird to tame, and so far, have not been successful with a white-breasted bird. This, of course, does not necessarily mean that *you* will be unable to tame one.

In the fall of 1936, I went on a deer-hunting trip in northern New Hampshire. This country is wild and beautiful, and at that time deer were so plentiful that you could jump one and if he was not just what you wanted, you could pass him up and wait until you found one that was. For almost three hours I had been jumping nothing but large and small fawn. I was tired and hungry, so I sat on a blowdown to rest and eat a lunch. I had taken a bite on a cheese sandwich when a white-breasted nuthatch settled on the blowdown, looked at me, and said: "Yank—yank—yank." I held out the sandwich and said: "Hello, little fellow, want a bite?" The bird studied me for a few seconds, then flew to my thumb, hung upside-down, and went to work. He did not bother with the bread but went right after the cheese. I knew he would not have come to me unless some other bird lover had hand-tamed him.

I walked a woods road back to the camp of the guide, Vic Ferguson, for dinner that evening. When I asked him if anyone near-by had been hand-taming birds, he said: "Sure, I have a lot of tame animals and birds around."

I told him about my failure in trying to tame white-breasted nuthatches, but he said he had had no trouble at all with them.

**RED-BREASTED NUTHATCH**

Here at Great Pond, I have had both white-breasted and red-breasted birds at my feeders, and although I have spent a great many hours trying to hand-tame both, I have been successful only with the red-breasted.

Many times, while finches fed on my hand, nuthatches would be at my feet picking up pieces of sunflower seed they dropped. One white-breasted bird even climbed up my pants for a few inches, but I could not coax him to my hand.

One bright morning when the temperature was twenty below, the suet in the woodpecker hole froze so hard that the chickadees were having a tough time chipping it out. I chopped some fresh suet to about the size of the head of a match and held it out. The birds came immediately. A female red-breasted nuthatch had been trying to get a meal out of the frozen fat too, but was not making out very well. She clung to the log-feeder as still as a rock while she watched the chickadees come and go.

When my fingertips got white and a little hard, I went into the house and rubbed them with cold water until I got some feeling back into them. I had a good breakfast of porcupine liver, bacon, and coffee and got warmed up, then went out to try again.

This time I made it; the nuthatch came over to the log feeder and watched a chickadee take a piece of suet. She clung to the log as she had before, upside-down, with her eyes never leaving the food on my hand. I watched her carefully for the little pulselike movement of her throat which would mean that her mouth was watering for the tasty bit I offered her. My fingers were getting just about all the weather they could take and I was about to quit for a while, when her throat throbbed. I stayed right there, and in a few seconds she flew close to my hand, fluttered like a hummingbird, dove in, and grabbed a piece of suet on the wing.

I went quickly into the house and rubbed my fingers again in cold water and had another cup of coffee. The nuthatch was back on the log a second after I went out again. This time she did not hesitate, but came right to my hand and took another piece of suet on the wing. Twice more that day she took suet the same way.

The following morning the temperature was much higher — a nice comfortable ten above. I started right in again with the nuthatch, but this time I held a walnut-sized piece of suet. I figured she would have a tough time trying to chip a piece of that while on the wing, and would have to settle on my hand or on the piece of suet if she wanted to eat. She settled on the food and chipped away at it. In a few seconds she was on my thumb. She immediately let go and flew to the log feeder, but was soon back. Now she ate without the slightest sign of fear. After that it was easy. When the other red-breasted nuthatches saw the little hen feeding on my hand, they knew it was safe and joined her.

Although white-breasted nuthatches have watched the smaller red-breasted birds feed on my hand, they have not come near. There have never been more than two of them at my feeder, and since the fall of 1961 I have seen only one of these two.

I have never tried to hand-tame a white-breasted nuthatch anywhere but here at Great Pond and wonder if these particular birds have at some time been handled. I have found that a banded bird will never come to the hand. There have been several at my feeder. Each time, although others in the flock would hand-tame, the banded bird would not even come near me. One large old male chickadee has been a steady boarder at my feeder for eight years. He will come no closer than a foot from my hand, and then the feathers stand up on his head and he keeps up a constant chatter the whole time he is near me. This chickadee is called "Grouchy Gramp" by the neighbors' children, whom I have taught how to hand-tame birds. Gramp is a banded bird.

# 6

The pine grosbeak, in my opinion, is the most gentle and tamest wild bird of them all. A few minutes before I started typing this page, I stood at the window of the kitchen door to watch chickadees, redpolls, red-breasted nuthatches, and pine gros-beaks at my feeders. There is about a foot of snow on the ground, and more is falling. There are about thirty tiny redpolls and seven grosbeaks on the two-foot feeder of the fir tree. The redpolls are crawling between the feet of the grosbeaks, picking up chips of sunflower seed and millet. A chickadee dives in now and then and grabs a sunflower seed. The grosbeaks are packed like sardines; they scold the red-polls, but although the tiny birds are rapidly cleaning up the food while fighting among themselves, the grosbeaks do not drive them away.

**PINE GROSBEAK** *and his friend, Al Martin*

The grosbeak is so beautiful that it is impossible to describe him accurately enough to do him justice. Vary-ing shades of reds, greens, and grays appear to contrast and yet melt into a beautiful soft harmony. No two males have exactly the same coloring. The females also vary consider-ably. A mature male may be a rich, deep orange, or almost any shade of red up to a dark reddish purple. A female may be almost blue, with a rich yellow head. You never can tell what color combination you will see when a strange flock comes in.

Unfortunately for a great many bird lovers, the pine grosbeak seldom goes to well-populated areas and is

**39**

more often seen at feeders in rural sections — and even there, he seldom shows.

The first two years I lived here at Great Pond, I watched my feeders every chance I had and always kept my ears open for the note of a grosbeak, but none came, and the only notes I heard were from the woods a long way off.

Finally, one midwinter morning I heard pine grosbeaks in my wood lot not more than five or six hundred yards from the house. The following morning the ground was covered with a few inches of snow. When I went out to brush off the feeders, I could hear the grosbeaks again, and a little closer than they were the day before. I filled all my pockets with sunflower seed and was soon standing near a larch tree watching a small flock of the birds picking at the branch tips. I sprinkled about a pound of seed on the snow near the tree and then stepped back to see if they would come down for it.

Five or six birds were in the tree, and one of them flew to a small fir not five feet from me. He looked me over but paid no attention to the seed. I left, and went back later. They had eaten all of the seed.

That same evening, just before dusk, I took a five-pound bag of seed down to the larch, sprinkled a little under the tree, then started back to the house, leaving a thin trail behind me as I walked. By the time I reached the big maple that grows about fifty yards from the house, I had about two ounces of seed left; this I put under the maple.

The following morning, the seed under and near the larch tree was gone; so was that under the maple, but the seed that trailed in plain view from the edge of the woods to the maple was still there. A little later I heard a grosbeak call. I was in the house so I knew the bird was pretty close. I quietly opened the kitchen door to listen; he was in the big maple. Most of the seed in the field had been eaten. I put some under the maple and trailed the rest to my feeders. That evening, just before dusk, I overloaded my window feeder with seed. The following morning I had three cock and two hen pine grosbeaks peeking at me through the window while they had a hearty breakfast.

I now started to get acquainted with my new friends. Every time I heard grosbeaks, I would leave the house and poke around, gradually getting closer to them. I always had sunflower seeds with me and when I was sure a bird was watching me I would slowly take some from my pocket and let it fall gently through my fingers. I kept this up until the birds were used to seeing me around, and then I started the actual hand-taming. The very same method is used for these as was used for the chickadees.

Many people believe that birds do not reason and cannot remember anything. Some give them credit for a tiny bit of memory and reason. A top naturalist friend once told me that the smartest bird could not remember an event for more than a year. I later discovered that the pine grosbeak can remember some things for at least two years. He can remember where my feeders are located, and he can remember to tap on my window pane if he finds no food on them. He also remembers me.

Pine grosbeaks and redpolls do not return every year, as the other birds do. Grosbeaks will return to the feeder for five or six years and then fail to show up the following year.

When this first happened, I was very much disturbed. I thought of my pets being eaten by predators or pounded to death in a violent hailstorm. I thought I would have to go to the trouble of tolling new, strange grosbeaks to the feeder as I had the first ones. But there were none to be seen anywhere. Nobody I knew had seen one of the birds that winter.

A year passed, then one snowy January morning, soon after dawn, there was a tap on my window. I looked around and a female grosbeak was hanging on the window beading while she flapped her wings and pecked at the pane. I immediately went to the door with a cereal dish full of sunflower seed, and before I could step outside she was on the bowl. Another one settled on my head and two more were on the steps. I heard others up in the apple tree. Two years before, fifteen hand-tamed grosbeaks had left the feeder; now only four of them returned, but they had remembered, and they had four new birds with them. When they left, late in March, they were all hand-tamed.

The words I use while taming grosbeaks are: "Come and get it, come and get it." When I call in the birds, I always use the same tone as used at the feeder, but louder, of course. You will notice that I use a different set of words for each specie, and that each set is a command. Even when a grosbeak is on my hand I keep saying: "Come and get it." This is important, because the bird gets to know that your call means food.

If you should be hidden in thick foliage and wish to call a grosbeak, he will come to you only if you use the same tone of voice and the same words. A tame hungry chickadee may be closer to you than the bird you are calling, but if he cannot see you he will not come to your grosbeak call, because he does not understand it; the grosbeak will not come to the chickadee call under the same conditions. If you should train different species of birds to come to the same call, you would have a tough time feeding any of them; they would all come together and fight. They would knock all the seed off your hand, and few of them would get anything at all to eat.

The tone of voice used in training and calling a bird is even more important than the wording.

A few years back, I had a pet raven. "Poe" was without exception the most intelligent wild bird I have ever known. Before she was three months old she could understand and obey many commands and would retrieve a tossed stick as well as any dog.

My good friends Andrew and Florence Wittrup of Franklin, Massachusetts, drove into my drive just as Poe came hopping up to me with a stick in her bill one day. They sat in the car and watched in amazement as I threw the stick again and Poe went after it, brought it back, and dropped it at my feet.

Andy asked if he could try it, so I gave him the stick and stepped back to watch. He waved it a little, then threw it. He turned to Poe and said: "Go fetch!" The bird did not move. Andy repeated the command, but Poe just sat looking up at him. She had not understood a word he said. Andy tried again, without success. I said: "Go get it, Poe; bring it back." She instantly obeyed the command. Andy asked me to do it again and Poe retrieved it the second time. Then Andy tried once more, but again without success.

If he had used the same words I had and the same tone of voice, Poe would have obeyed his command. If I had used Andy's words and tone, she would not have obeyed me.

Let us get back to the pine grosbeak.

One morning I heard a flock of them kicking up a fuss so I went out to see what was troubling them and found a female grosbeak in the grip of a weasel. I yelled as loud as I could and rushed at him. He dropped her, but bit through her wing bone near the shoulder before he bounded to a near-by rock pile and sat snapping his teeth at me.

The bird lay on her side with the damaged wing spread out like a fan; her eyes were closed and she was breathing heavily. I spoke to her and she opened her eyes and looked at me. I picked her up very carefully and held her with a firm grip for fear she might struggle from my hand, but she knew me and understood she was safe. Her heartbeat became slower, and she did not try to move at any time while I held her. If she had not been tame she might have struggled and caused further damage to her wing.

The broken wing of a small bird is difficult to handle, and more often than not, she can make a better recovery by tending to it alone. I decided to give this one the chance.

Holding her in one hand, I prepared a small cage for her with the other. I took all the perches out, put in some gravel, placed a few pieces of bark and a coffee-jar top filled with water in one corner, and sprinkled sunflower seed close to the water and bark. I then hung the cage on the kitchen wall where it was away from any draft, and put the bird in, close to the bark.

She looked the cage over carefully, ate a few seeds, took a drink, and arranged her damaged wing on a piece of bark. She looked at me, then tucked her little green head under her good wing and went to sleep.

She stayed in that corner for two days. I did not bother her at all; in fact, I did not even change the drinking water for fear she might hurt her healing wing. But I

**44**

gave her more sunflower seed by holding a handful up over the cage and letting it fall gently into her corner.

Complete rest is very important to a sick bird. The only exercise this little hen had was the constant dressing of her wing. On the third day, she began moving about the cage a little, so I gave her fresh water and a container of buttermilk, a piece of apple, and fresh seed and gravel. The next day I put in a low perch, about an inch from the floor, so she could get up on it without moving her wings. She improved rapidly and inside of a week was able to get onto a higher perch. She kept right after her healing wing all the time, every five or ten minutes, and I could not help thinking how much more this tiny bird knew about setting and healing a broken wing than I did about a broken arm.

The little bird was now ready to test her wing. I took her outdoors.

Her first try was a little disappointing; she pointed her bill at the top of a small apple tree about twenty feet away and started out bravely, but hit the ground about ten feet from the tree. Back in the house again, she sat and dressed her wing, and spread it out a few times. She stretched all over, then took a nap.

The next morning I tried her again, and this time she did a little better; she landed about five feet from the tree. A few hours later, she tried again and landed at the base of it. The following morning she made a low branch of the tree from a distance of twenty feet. I walked over to her and she sat looking at me, and I feel pretty sure she thought she had done very well.

I hung her cage in the tree and wired it so that she could enter it easily. I put in plenty of food and a drinking fountain, and sat down to watch for a few moments.

**45**

She went directly into the cage, had a drink, then came out again. She hopped from one branch to another until she was well up in the tree.

The damaged wing of the grosbeak had set about one eighth of an inch lower than the other. This might bother her for a while, but she would take care of it by regulating the other wing and would soon get used to it. My only worry now was that a hawk might spot her, and that would be the end.

Just before dusk, I went out to the tree to see if I could call her into the cage. I heard a soft *peep*, and there she was, already safe for the night.

A few days later, the grosbeaks started to sing and pair off; the next day they were all gone except my little hen.

For the next two weeks the little bird exercised herself in my orchard. I watched her every day, and once she flew to the steeple of the old church. I have never seen another grosbeak settle on it, and I am sure the only reason she did so was to test the strength and coordination of her wings. The tip of the church spire is much higher than the tallest tree in the village.

Our local game warden, Ed Wuori, is a very good friend, not only to me but also to all wild creatures; he is very wise in Nature's ways. Ed and I were sitting at my kitchen window watching the lone grosbeak on the feeder, when she sat bolt upright and let out a loud call note. In a few seconds, a beautiful young male was singing and swaying his shoulders at the little hen. I guess she must have been very lonesome, because she took no chances on keeping him guessing for a while, but accepted him right away. He was a deep, rich orange.

**46**

For the next two weeks the little hen and the orange cock were the only pine grosbeaks seen in these parts. Then one morning, soon after dawn, the pair of birds stood on my hand facing me, but would not take a seed. They kept looking over their shoulders to the northwest while they kept up a steady run of warbling notes. They were not singing as the pine grosbeak sings, but were both making exactly the same sound, like softly gurgling water, only much sweeter. It resembled, in a way, the sad tone of the warning note of alarm of the grosbeak. Both birds kept this up about ten seconds, then looked down at the seed on my hand, but still did not touch it. They sat silent for a few seconds, and then took off. They headed northwest, flying side by side; the little hen was just as strong in the air as her beautiful orange mate.

An hour later I sat eating breakfast and looking at the feeder. I was already missing the little hen, but when I thought of what the bird had gone through, and how things had turned out for her, I felt mighty fine.

# 7

The purple finch is not easily tamed. I have found that only about three out of ten will come to the hand.

In every flock of these birds there is always at least one ill-tempered glutton, and this will always be the first to come to your hand. Every year I tame new finches, and the first one is always a female who will try to drive away any other bird who comes near me.

**PURPLE FINCHES**

*These birds know how to fight.*

Purple finches are great fighters; some are even killed while fighting over food. A male will usually give in to a female, but I once watched a female get a good hold on the back of a male's neck and spread her wings on the ground for support while he tried to pull back from her; the more the frightened male pulled, the harder the female pulled. Watching them closely, I noticed that she timed her pull with that of the male. She sat tight and if he did not pull, neither would she. She could have opened her bill and he would have flown off; but she wanted to have no more trouble with him. She wanted to scalp him, so she held right on to the back of his neck until in a final dash for freedom he was thoroughly scalped.

The unfortunate male stood there with the skin of the back of his neck and head hanging down over his bill like a red stocking. The female went back to eat more seed.

I pulled the skin back over the injured bird's head to its normal position, and put him in the casualty cage. The next morning he was dead; he had lost a lot of blood.

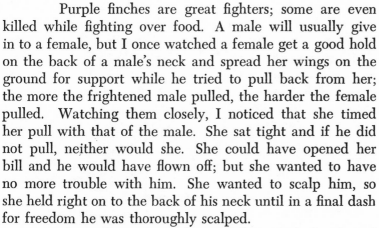

**49**

Other birds beside purple finches strive for the neck hold while in battle. The canary uses it if he gets the chance, and the Mexican red-headed linnet is so fond of using it that most aviaries shy away from this species.

A fight over food between two female purple finches is really a great show of skill, strength, speed, and courage. These fights usually take place when the food is cleaned up and one hen finds a leftover sunflower seed. It takes her a few seconds to crack it; another hen tries to steal it and then the fight is on. The first bird drops the seed and goes after the thief. They bang away at each other with wings, bills, and feet; over and over they go in the snow, both trying for the neck hold. Beating and banging, feathers all over the place, soon they have a good grip on each other; then, as if the bell had rung, they both lie motionless for a few seconds. Then they are at it again. Up they go, as high as thirty feet in the air, then down. Neither has lost her hold. They struggle on the snow for a few seconds, then still locked together, they lie quiet, panting. Sometimes they will go up in the air like this two or three times.

One of these fights lasted so long, and the birds looked so near death, that I walked out to separate them, with the intention of placing them in cages until they were healed up. When I was a few feet from them they both took off as if nothing had happened.

The purple finch is a very rugged little bird, and as far as I can tell, these fights between females always wind up as draws. Perhaps I have not seen enough of them, but I have watched at least a dozen such bouts, and in every fight the last round finished as a draw.

When females fight, neither bird tries to escape, but each gives the best she has. Fights between males and

**50**

females are altogether different; they start pounding each other for a few seconds, and then the male tries to escape. The female never does. If the hen has her favorite nape-hold the male is scalped. If she has any other hold, she will release the male after a brief struggle. A fight between male and female seldom lasts more than half a minute. Occasionally the male starts the fight, but it does not last. He starts in like a cyclone, but in a few seconds he says, "Yes, dear," and the fight is over.

Hand-taming the purple finch is done in the same way as with the chickadee. Purple finches learn to crack tough sunflower seeds, but it is best to use smaller seeds for them. They are very fond of flax, and you will have better luck and save time by using some of this in your mixture.

Purple finches and other seed-eating birds often get snared in shrubs and vines, especially in the spring. One of the birds I tamed came to me that way.

Early one beautiful spring morning in 1950, I started down into Union River Valley to see if I could pick up a few squaretail trout.

Hap Higgins had taken a few near the Rocky Narrows of the river; they were the first fish to be taken so far this spring. They were nice and fat, and looked very tasty. I could hardly wait to get a brace of them.

As I walked down the trail that winds through the beautiful valley, I began to wonder if any wrens had arrived yet. As if in answer to my thoughts, a wren rasped his little scolding note at me. The sun peeked over Archers' Hill, and in a few minutes the woods were full of music. The cedar swamp seemed full of wrens, and their glorious songs seemed to add even more color to the beautiful shades of sun-lit greens. I sat on an old, curved, white cedar log to listen to them, and to smoke a cigarette. I wondered

**51**

if the tiny birds were as happy as they sounded — but it seemed to me that no living thing could possibly be that happy.

I heard the *chip-chip* notes of flying purple finches as a flock went over the trees in back of me. Then I had that woodsman's feeling of a pair of eyes staring at the back of his head. I reached down to press my cigarette into the damp earth and saw the tiny one-inch tracks of a pair of baby fawns. I glanced behind me but could see no signs of the deer, although they were no more than fifteen feet from me. I knew the doe had told her babies not to move until she gave the word.

I started out again down the trail, which took a sharp turn to the right and went through a small clearing. As I approached it a flock of purple finches left the ground and headed toward the river. A few more yards took me to the spot where they had been feeding. A male bird had been left behind, all tangled up in a vine. I spoke to him, but he was scared and beat about with all the strength he had. I backed away from him and he slowed down a little; he soon had his wings free, but when he started up, one of his feet was still anchored, and his little leg snapped. It was time for me to take over and free him from the tangle. Holding him firmly, I put bird and hand in a pocket of my fishing jacket and started back home.

Soon a split feather-quill splint was on the bird's broken leg, and he lay panting on his side in the casualty cage. He was almost scared to death.

I had learned as a boy that if you can make a wild creature think you are scared of him, he immediately loses most of his fear of you, so I used the old trick Mr. Buckmaster had used to steady a wild bird.

I stretched out my arm with a finger pointing

**52**

directly at him, then very slowly walked to the cage. He sat up, watching my finger, and his poor little tummy was hitting the floor of the cage so rapidly I was afraid his heart would burst. I felt very sorry for him, but I knew his leg would not heal properly as long as he was afraid of me. When my finger was a few inches from the cage, I withdrew it as fast as I could. The bird's stomach slowed down considerably. I repeated the action, and this time the stomach throb was about normal. I went closer to the cage, and slowly pointed my finger at him with the cushion of it between the wires, and that did it. He spread his shoulders, opened his bill and was ready to fight, broken leg forgotten.

Left alone now, he settled down quietly to the business of eating, drinking, and sleeping, and healing his broken leg.

I fed him a mixture of rape, niger, flax, dandelion, small white millet, and canary seed, and put a large piece of apple in the cage. Every morning I gave him a small container of moist — not sloppy — bread and milk.

This purple finch became very tame and in a few days was singing as if he were the happiest bird in the world.

Over a week had passed since the splint was put on, and now I took it off to have a look. The leg had healed beautifully; unless you were looking for it, you would never have noticed the faint mark around the break.

The bird knew exactly what I was doing; he never moved a muscle as I took off the quill. Although he was very tame, when I released him he did not hesitate a second, but took right off for the west, and as I watched him turn into a tiny speck this side of Black Cap Mountain, I knew he would be with the rest of his flock before long.

A few years back, one of the neighborhood children came in with a male purple finch in his hand. He had seen him several times and had noticed that something was wrong with him because the bird never flew away when he got near it.

I looked the finch over, and apart from his being a little thin, I could see nothing wrong with him. I placed him on the kitchen floor and he hopped a few steps, then spread his wings. His right wing was all right, but the left one moved sideways over his back. I put some seed and water on the floor. He drank about three times the amount ordinarily taken by a purple finch, and then went to work on the seed. The poor little fellow was half starved.

I left him in the kitchen that night and in the morning he was sitting on the low rung of a chair about ten inches from the floor. He was sound asleep. He did not wake up when I turned on the lights, but slept while I cooked and ate my breakfast. I went out in the yard to listen to the birds, as I always do in nice weather just before dawn.

Fifteen minutes later when I went back into the house, the finch was on the floor feeding. I waited until he had finished his meal, then picked him up and examined his left wing, but still could see nothing wrong with it. The bones were all right. I put him back on the floor and he looked perfect; both wings seemed set in normal position.

I had been working on a rather difficult oil painting when the little boy came in with the finch the day before. This picture was to show two whitetail deer in shallow water at dawn. If you are a painter, you may agree with me that unless you can work in full, uninterrupted concentration, your picture may look more like that of a smoldering forest fire than a scene of early morning mist.

**54**

I worked in my attic to avoid interruption, but left all doors open so that I could hear if company arrived.

When I went down later for lunch on this particular day and looked around for the purple finch, he was nowhere to be seen. I searched every room on the ground floor, but the bird had disappeared completely. I placed fresh seed and water on the floor and felt sure he would come to it before the day was over, but he did not.

Early the next morning I was back at the painting again. A purple finch was singing close to the back of the house. I worked along steadily until lunch time. The seed and water had still not been touched.

I asked some of the children if they had seen anyone come to the house the day before, but they had not.

The following day I spent a few more hours on the painting and again heard the song of a purple finch outside. Soon after dark, rain began spattering down heavily, and I went upstairs to close the windows. The purple finch sang again. I knew now that the little bird was in the house and was singing to let me know where.

With lights on full, plus a flashlight, I searched every inch of that side of the attic where the song came from. In one corner there were several rustic stumps and branches I kept for taxidermy work, and these were piled up to the top of the sheet-rock wall about eight feet from the floor. The room had not been finished, and every sixteen inches along the top of the sheet-rock there was a six-inch air space between the upright supports. These spaces went clean to the floor, and I wondered if it were possible for the little bird to have climbed up those branches and fallen into one of them.

The attic is a large room and the sheet-rock was well nailed to the studding, and to make matters worse,

**55**

most of the studs were hemlock, which is tough wood to draw nails from.

I was wondering just what to do in order to get to the little bird before he starved to death, when I remembered that he always sang just as I entered the room.

I went down to the kitchen for seed and water and came in again. The little fellow went into song as I entered, and I was able to come pretty close to him before he stopped. With a jackknife in hand I crawled along the floor to where he seemed to be; then I remembered that when I gave him his first water and seed, I had said: "There, little fellow." Now I said the same thing in the same tone, and believe me, my eyes were pretty moist when that little fellow burst into song.

I went to work with my knife on the sheet-rock close to the floor, and once I almost cut the finch, for as soon as the hole was big enough for his little red head, he poked it right out. I had to finish the job with one finger in the hole to keep him away from the knife.

The instant I took my finger away, he was out and at the water. He ate a few seeds and then went into a sound sleep, sitting on the edge of the coffee jar lid that contained them. Rather than disturb him, I covered him with a half-bushel basket, put a light blanket over the basket, and left him there.

At daylight the following morning, I took up a large cage with seed, buttermilk, and gravel. The seed was sprinkled on the floor just inside the open door. When I lifted the basket the finch was wide awake but showed no sign of fear. He stretched himself, went right into the cage, took a drink, and went to work on the seed.

While the little fellow was shelling out the seed, something was bothering me, and I could not understand

**56**

why. I was still a little sleepy myself. Then I had it; when the bird had stretched himself, both wings had functioned normally! But he was too weak to turn loose yet.

I hung the cage on the kitchen wall, and the bird hopped to the highest perch, using both wings in the flip-hop. In the week that followed, he gained rapidly and filled my kitchen with music. He seemed to have no desire for freedom, but it was mating time, so I hung the cage outside with the door open. He hopped to the doorframe then went back to his favorite perch. He stayed in the cage all day until just before dusk, when a small flock of purples came into the yard.

There were seven in the flock, and two of them settled on the cage for a second and then flew to the ground. The little fellow took a drink first, then joined the others. I left the cage hanging outdoors, and the next morning it was full of purple finches! I shooed them out and took down the cage, and in a few days the birds were too busy to come back.

What the trouble was with that purple finch's left wing I never did discover. Somehow while imprisoned or while falling into that sheet-rock trap he regained the full use of it. A muscle must have been out of place; whatever it was, he probably would have died if that little boy had not noticed him. He certainly would have died if he had not sung while trapped. I am sure he sang to ask for help; he certainly did not sing because he was happy!

Another thing I have wondered about is why the bird made the long trip up my attic stairs. Did he know that he was helpless without the use of both wings? Did he feel safe while he was near a human who had given him food and water? I think so.

# 8

The redpoll is a little bit shy at first, but is not difficult to tame. Unlike the purple finch, most redpolls will quickly come to your hand or settle on your head and shoulders. Once you get the first bird to come, you will soon be covered with them.

**REDPOLLS** *are easy to tame.*

I do not have redpolls at my feeders every year. In the past ten years, they have come only four times.

My feeders had been set up for three years before the first flock came. There were about a dozen, and they all landed in my driveway. No seed was on the feeder; it was still dawn when the birds came in. I was afraid to open the kitchen door to put out food, because I knew they would take off as soon as the door moved. I stood watching them and wondering how I could manage without scaring them. It was much lighter now, and a blue jay came sailing in and landed in the middle of the redpolls. They went up in every direction, and one young cock smacked right into the window of the kitchen door.

I watched him for a second, but he seemed to be all right. He shook himself, then let out his canary-like call note, and almost immediately the flock were on the steps. Some of them found a few small millet seed, and then the jay came back and scared them off again.

I cursed the jay, but this did give me a chance to throw a handful of seed on the feeder. The redpolls soon came back for it, and a week later, I had one of them feeding from my hand.

Not long after this, we had some mean, cold weather. It was too cold outside for me, so I got a good fire going in the wood stove, bundled up in the warmest clothing I could find, and sprinkled seed on the kitchen floor. Then I invited the redpolls in to dinner.

About forty of them came inside. They were everywhere, and the racket they made sounded like a million instead of forty birds.

Most of them fed on the floor; some were poking their worried-looking faces into cups, pans, glasses, and open bags of groceries. One little cock landed on the top of the hot cooking stove, where he bounced up and down, up and around and down again, then took a complete somersault and rolled off, and quick as a flash flew to the antlers of a mounted deer head. He lifted one foot, bent his head down to get a good look at it, picked it a little, then did the same to the other foot. His actions were more like those of a little mouse than a bird.

I watched carefully, but in a minute he was on the floor feeding with the others and appeared to be all right.

The redpolls stayed about ten minutes, then in an instant they were all gone.

The next day was even colder. I was up long before dawn, and before any birds arrived I had seed on the fir-tree feeder and some on the window slab.

Dawn was just breaking when the redpolls came. I was sitting by the kitchen window eating breakfast, and my mind was far away in a tropical land, when a great black cloud landed like a flash at the window, just like a twister, and I almost jumped out of my chair. The forty birds I had in the kitchen the day before must have invited every red-

60

poll they could find; there were at least two hundred of them.

The pound of seed I had already put out lasted just about long enough for me to finish breakfast. I spread two pounds more over the kitchen table, poured myself another cup of coffee, and lifted the window a few inches, then sat down to enjoy the show. Every bird took off when I lifted the window, but they were back again in a minute. In they came, all over the table, on my shoulders and head, one hanging on my left ear, two on the other, while several of them were climbing up my neck, then sliding down again. Some were flying around the room; they were on the deer head, in among the dishes on the sideboard; they were everywhere. I reached for my cup of coffee and a little hen settled on the rim of the cup. She sat looking at me for a few seconds, then turned around to give me a good view of the feathers under her tail. She lifted it a little higher and dropped her card right into my coffee, turned to face me and said *"Peep,"* then joined the others to feed on the table.

The birds soon cleaned up the seed and went out as quickly as they had come in. Although there had been about two hundred in the room, not another one landed on the stove or went very close to it. Maybe they could feel the heat when they got near it. Or perhaps they had been told to keep away from it. I wouldn't know — would you?

These birds were lesser redpolls. I have never had a flock of greater redpolls at my feeder in Maine, but a single one did come in with a flock of the smaller birds. This was one of the most beautiful birds I have ever seen.

The first time I saw him, I thought he was a white hawk, but only for a split second. The bird was two hundred yards away and flying along behind a flock of red-polls. They were flying fast but in normal formation, and the white bird seemed to be having a tough time keeping up with them. The flock soon disappeared behind some tall pines, and I did not see them again for two days.

The next time I saw these birds they were all at my feeder, and the big white one was in the middle of them. He was not pure white as he had appeared at a distance with sun shining on him, but a beautiful shade of vermilion; streaks on his breast were salmon pink; his bill was a pale yellow-pink and all underparts were as white as snow.

This beautiful creature was the prize glutton of the flock. He would not allow one of the others near him while he ate seed as fast as he could get it down. I wondered if his craving for food had caused him to leave his own kind so that he could always get the lion's share.

The following morning the redpolls dropped in again, and the pink bird was so heavy he could hardly fly. He would soon be dead unless he went on a diet, and I knew he would not do that, so I decided to help him out.

I put some flax, rape, and millet seed in one of the little trap-cages I had brought back from England, set the trap on the snow under the window feeder, and sprinkled a very few seeds on the snow. Then I went inside to watch.

No call bird was needed, because the redpolls would come back for food anyway. All I had to do was make sure there was no other seed available except the few on the snow and a lot on the feeder of the trap-cage. The pink bird would grab the cage, because most of the food was there.

In a few minutes they came in, with Pinky struggling along behind. All the birds settled on the feeder to pick up what few seeds remained in the crevices of the bark. Pinky was not with them, he was already in the trap. When I took him out, he felt like a hot, hard-boiled egg.

There was still time to save him. I had already prepared a cage for him with plenty of fresh gravel, a pinch of epsom salts in the drinker, a large piece of apple between wires in one side, and no seed.

Pinky beat around a bit in the cage; so I gave him the "finger works," and he soon settled down.

The next morning he looked very unhappy. He sat on the perch all puffed up. As I approached him those beautiful vermilion feathers on top of his head stood up like a waxwing's. He had been having visions of starving to death, and he was mad clean through. I gave him a mixture of eight parts small white millet, one part rape, and one part dandelion seed. He was not yet tame, but he was so hungry that he was at the seed before I had the dispenser firmly seated. He picked away at it, taking only the rape, and tossing the rest on the floor of the cage. The following morning I put a little less rape seed in the mixture. This kept up until in a few days there was nothing for him to eat but millet, dandelion seed, and apple. Pinky had no intention of going hungry so he ate what he was given.

About twice a day I would put three or four flax seeds on the cushion of my finger, and Pinky would pick them off. He became very tame and he also was losing weight. He loved to take a bath and sometimes took two the same day. I put in his bath every morning at about ten, and he looked forward to it and knew almost the exact minute he would get it.

One morning some early visitors sat at the table with me, swapping fishing lies. One of the fellows stood

**63**

up to demonstrate the way he had handled an Atlantic salmon on the first run. As he pushed back his chair, Pinky began cheeping and beating his wings against the wire. The fisherman instantly stopped his demonstration and said he was sorry he had frightened the bird. I told him not to worry, that it must be ten o'clock and Pinky was asking for his bath. We all looked at the clock; it was three minutes past ten. The three men stared at each other; they found this hard to believe. I spoke to Pinky, then put his bath in the cage. He was in it before I had time to place it on the floor.

I never refused Pinky his bath. No matter what I was working on, as soon as he peeped and beat his wings, I dropped everything and gave it to him.

In another week he was in excellent condition, singing every hour or so, and was ready to join his friends. I waited for the flock to come in, then took out the cage with Pinky in it. But he did not want to leave. The game warden drove in just then and joined me on the doorstep. Pinky would not leave the cage. I did not wish to force him, and hoped he would stay around, but it was time for him to be out of the cage. I placed him on the ground and closed the door. He tried to squeeze back in through the wire. I took the cage into the house.

Pinky sat on the ground looking at me; he did not move a muscle, and I got that little pang of remorse all bird lovers feel when they unavoidably hurt a pet.

The husky warden also felt it. He smiled and gently shook his head. A few minutes later, a flock of redpolls went over in the east. Pinky let out three loud call notes, but the flock did not come in. He let out one more call, then like a flash, he headed into the east. He never came back.

**64**

# 9

I have found catbirds hard to tame. There are fewer to work with, and they do not come in flocks.

My lot takes in twenty-five acres of mixed country suitable for cat-birds, but there have never been more than two nesting pairs on my land at one time.

**CATBIRD**

*Extra patience is called for with this specie.*

A catbird seems to get along very well with other species, but does not like another catbird near its nest.

They are great hiders, and although their bright gray coloring stands out sharply when they are not hidden in the brush, it is almost impossible to see one if there are two or three small leaves in front of it.

It is hard to see a mother catbird when she is on her nest. I have, on more than one occasion, parted the branches of a shrub or small tree, looking for one, and not seen the bird until she moved a few inches from my hand. A catbird will sit on a branch and serenade you, but as soon as his song is finished he will keep out of sight as much as he can.

If you have no thickly-branched trees or shrubs near your feeder, you have little chance of hand-taming one of these birds.

Although his food is something like that of the robin, he will not come to your lawn for it; he will not seek his food in the open unless he is forced to.

The grounds surrounding my house are covered with trees and shrubs. I have no cultivated flowers; my

lawn is never cut, and wild flowers seed on it to feed the
wild birds. I planted fir, spruce, pine, and hemlock around
my circular drive, and every season you can find nests in
them.

Two large thick shrubs are at the southwest corner
of the house; one is lilac, the other a syringa bush. On the
northwest corner there is another syringa bush; old-fashioned roses and long grass grow in the center. When a
catbird comes for food, he always takes full advantage of
this cover, going from bush to bush, carefully keeping out
of sight as much as he can until he reaches the feeder. As
soon as he gets what food he needs, he flies boldly away
through the air in the direction of his nest. But he does
not go straight to it; he stops a hundred feet or more from
it. He carefully looks the place over first. Even after he
is satisfied that everything is all right, he keeps out of sight
as much as he can while approaching the nest.

Seed, of course, cannot be used for these fruit and
insect-eating birds. I have found that the dark-colored
seedless raisins and cooking currants do the job nicely.

If you have catbirds on your property, it is more
likely than not that they never show at your feeder. Mine
had been in operation for five years before the first catbird came to them. When my back kitchen window was
open, I could often hear the birds singing but seldom got
a glimpse of them. They kept away from the front yard and
never came close to the house.

After my success in tolling the pine grosbeaks to the
feeder I could see no reason why the same method would
not work for catbirds. I walked out back and searched for
their nest and finally found it in a small fir tree. It was,
as usual, very well hidden, and it contained three eggs.
Both birds screamed at me, so I backed away about twenty

feet. I sat on the ground and took a few raisins from my pocket and flicked them, one by one, as close to the nesting tree as I could. One of the raisins dropped on a flat rock and stayed there. I sat a few minutes more, but neither bird went for the food.

The nest was about two hundred yards from the feeder, and the ground for the first fifty yards was covered with tall weeds and blackberry, blueberry, wild raspberry and other puckerbrush (a local term used to describe any low-growing, bushy plant, such as sage, azalea, etc.). Pine, hemlock, fir, white birch, maple, and beech rose out of this thick carpet. If I wanted catbirds at the feeder I would have to do some work.

The following morning I started at the flat rock near the nesting tree and cleared a small patch about three feet square. About twenty feet toward the house I made another small clearing, and continued along with this plan until I was out of the puckerbrush. I then hunted up some flat rocks and flat pieces of bark or old weathered wood and placed one in the center of each little clearing, with a raisin on each.

The next day the raisin on the flat rock near the nest was gone; so were the next three, but the rest remained. I left things as they were, and the following day the only raisins left were the two nearest the house. I now dropped a raisin every few yards up to the front of the house. Robins love raisins, too. They would pick them up as fast as I put them down in the front yard. There were three pairs who came to the feeder at this time, so I put out enough raisins to last them for an hour, before trailing a few from the feeder to where the last two I had set out for the catbirds remained.

The following morning a male catbird was on my doorstep. He was very timid. He came to the feeder about once an hour. He would eat one raisin and take two away with him. I always made it a point to look first to make sure he was not at the feeder when I wished to open the kitchen door. Two weeks passed before I could get within fifteen feet of him, but by then he had lost most of his fear and he was ready for hand-taming. In a few days, he was taking raisins from my hand.

I had seen the hen only three or four times, but now the birds were taking turns coming to the feeder. The hen was not as nervous as the male had been, and would come close to me for a raisin, but she would not come to my hand. I would place a few raisins on one end of the feeder and rest my hand on the other end; she would snatch a raisin, then another, until she had four, then she would take off. I had not gone near the nest since the time I looked at it and saw the three eggs; she must have laid at least one more.

Both birds consistently ate the first raisin, then carried four away. I wondered what would happen if the hen could find only *three* raisins on the feeder, but could see another one on the palm of my hand. I waited to hear her sing, as she now did when asking for raisins, and at the first sound I put down my paint brush and went to the feeder with five raisins. I put four on the edge of the feeder and held the other one on the tip of my fingers. She came immediately and ate the first raisin; she picked up the other three, then sat as still as a statue looking at the one I held. She watched that raisin for at least half a minute and did not move a muscle, then she went down and looked for another raisin under the fir tree. She came back to the feeder, then like a flash took the raisin while on the wing.

**68**

After this it was easy; she came directly to my hand. It made no difference if I stood near the feeder or a hundred yards in the woods; she always knew where I was and would come to a call if I wanted her.

The cock still came to my hand too, but the hen was much tamer and had more nerve, so I concentrated on her.

The neighbor's children had named the catbirds. The male was called Cockie, the female, Kitty.

One day I was sitting on my steps tossing out raisins to the robins, when Kitty landed about ten feet from me. I tossed out a raisin and she caught it just before it hit the ground. I flicked the next one into the air and she went up after it. This was the beginning of a little game that Kitty loved to play. I would flick a raisin as high into the air as I could, and the instant it left my hand she would leave the ground, and she would have the raisin before it started to fall.

One day I tried to fool her. I made the motion of flicking a raisin into the air but held on to it. Kitty was not fooled a bit; she did twitch her shoulders, but that was all. I tried it again to see what she would do, and this time she hopped around flapping her wings and tail, looking first at me, then up in the air. I tossed up a raisin and she went up after it, and as before, got it before it started down. Kitty obviously enjoyed this little game, because from that time on, she never went to the feeder for raisins, but would sing for me to go out and toss them up for her. I would hear her singing in the fir tree and by the time I got outside with the raisins she would be on the ground dancing around and flapping her wings.

Another day I lay spread-eagled, taking a sun bath, and was half asleep when there was a fluttering directly over my face. I paid no attention to it for a second or two and then I could feel the breeze on my face. I opened my eyes and there was Kitty hovering over me, hanging in the air like a hawk. I spoke to her and she instantly flew to a chokecherry bush and burst into the loudest, shrillest song I ever heard from the throat of a catbird. I am positive she thought she had lost her meal ticket and was overjoyed when she discovered I was not dead.

Before long the catbirds had their second brood, and Cockie and Kitty were again carrying raisins to their babies.

One morning Kitty did not come for her raisins, and I was worried. Then as the day wore on and Cockie came more often to the feeder, I knew that Kitty must be disabled or dead. I asked one of the children if he had seen her and he told me that he and another boy had seen a cat leave my steps with a grey bird in her mouth. Kitty did not show up the rest of that day.

I got very little sleep that night. I kept thinking about her. I made some coffee and sat at the window listening to heavy rain pattering on the glass. It was one A.M., so I picked up a book and tried to read but fell asleep in the chair.

The next day Cockie was missing, and it was not until the following day that I found out the same cat had taken him. A boy saw her leaving my driveway and he could see she had a catbird in her mouth.

I had not bothered the pair and had not seen the second nest, but I had a good idea where it was. Now that I knew for sure that both birds were dead, I wanted to save the babies; but it was too late. They were all cold, wet, and dead by the time I found them. I am not exactly a softy, but when I looked at those dead babies and thought of their wonderful, trusting parents, it was very hard to keep from crying like a child. Living alone as I do, it was like losing some of my family.

I was so upset that I cannot remember a thing from the time I left the dead baby birds, until I found myself in the living room of the Fred Williams family, who owned the cat. I insulted them thoroughly, and although they had no idea at first what it was all about, they reciprocated beautifully; they defended their cat as they should, and after a while I cooled down. I realized I could no more hold them responsible for her actions than I could blame the cat for doing what Nature intended. The Williams are wonderful people and I value their friendship. I apologized for my rude intrusion and left the house.

Something had to be done if I wanted to save my birds. The cat had discovered a hunting paradise of well-fed birds and would lie hidden at dawn and dusk; she would kill at least two birds a day as long as the supply lasted.

There seemed nothing I could do about it. The cat had had all the best of food she needed at home, but she was a great hunter. I could very easily dispose of her, but I like cats too, and even if I disliked them, I could never hurt the pet of a friend — or any pet, for that matter. There seemed to be only one thing to do: give up the hobby and pastime I loved the best. I pulled down all my feeders and put out no more seed, and in a few days the birds no longer came. With no more birds at the feeder, the cat looked for greener pastures.

I had no more birds for the rest of that year.

**10**

Ruby-throat hummingbirds steal the
show at my feeders, though some
children appear to get more kick out
of a hand-tamed chipmunk than they
do from all the birds put together.
Hummingbirds do not actually take
food from your fingers. It would
be difficult to entice one to your hand with syrup on it,
because your hand does not in any way resemble the kind
of plant that might contain nectar as he sees it. Any of
the small syrup holders used today do in a way resemble
flowers. You may occasionally have one of these birds settle
on your thumb or finger and sit there for a minute or so,
then drink from the feeder in your hand.

**RUBY-
THROATED
HUMMING-
BIRD**

*Small enough to
ride a goose (a
hundred humming-
birds would weigh
less than twelve
ounces)*

For feeders use any kind of container that is no
larger than an inch and a half in diameter and deep enough
to hold at least a tablespoon of syrup. Opinion varies as to
the best color; I have found that yellow gives the best results. A friend who is very successful with hummingbirds
will use nothing but red.

A lot depends on how early you put out your syrup
cups. I now put mine out long before the hummingbirds
arrive. One spring a ruby-throat came in at least a week
early. I had no syrup out for him, and he did not stay. He
was not one of the tame birds, because he did not buzz the
kitchen window as they will do if the cups are empty.

As soon as the cliff swallows appear I put out the
syrup cups. One is hung on the side of the house near
the kitchen window, and the other on a five-foot stick, set

in the roots of day lilies on the south side of the house. This set-up makes it easy for visitors to take pictures of the birds, and when the day lilies are in bloom they make a nice background.

I never use more than two feeders because in my estimation that gives the birds enough sugar. Some bird fans use watered honey instead of sugar. They feel that too much sugar is harmful, and it is, just as too much peanut butter is harmful to chickadees. But I have been feeding sugar to hummingbirds for fifty years and have kept them under close observation. I have never seen one leave a feeder without going on directly to flowers to feed on nectar and insects. There seem to be no ill effects from the sugar.

For syrup, two teaspoons of sugar to a standard cup of water is thick enough to attract tiny insects, and not too thick for the birds.

Do not fill your syrup cups to overflowing. If the least drop of syrup is spilled on the ground, your feeder will soon be full of ants who will drink up the syrup or drown in the attempt, and the hummingbirds will not go near it. The cups should be cleaned every evening at dusk, filled to within one half inch of the brim, and put out for the early birds at dawn.

As is the case with all wild creatures, some hummingbirds are very bold; others are quite timid. Some take a long time to tame; others can be coaxed to the hand in less than an hour. You will most likely find that the males are easier to tame than the females, but compared to other birds both are easy.

When hummingbirds have been coming to your feeders for a week and have seen you in the offing each time, you will be ready to start taming them.

Sit or stand, but be sure you are comfortable, close

to your feeder. Keep as still as you can and wait for the bird to come. When he sees you near his syrup, he may try to drive you away; he may swoop down at you and almost hit you on the head. Sit perfectly still, he has no intention of striking you. He may try this a few times. He is very fast but all he wants to do is come as close to your head as he can. If you should duck quickly you might just possibly get your head in exactly the same spot where he had decided to pass, and you would feel as though you were hit by a truck — and he would most likely break his little neck. As long as you stay still, you have nothing to fear.

After buzzing you a few times, the hummingbird will most likely fly to a near-by perch to watch you and think the matter over. If you have not moved, he will come over to the feeder, buzz back and forth, to and from it, while he keeps one eye on you and the other on the feeder. Then he will shoot into the feeder, take a very quick taste, and back out again to see what you are doing. He will do this three or four times, but each time he takes a little more syrup, until he is hanging in the air taking a good drink.

After you have gone through this whole procedure twice, the bird will probably come straight to the feeder without fear. The next time he comes in you should be directly in back of the feeder, with your thumb and index finger resting on the bottom of the syrup cup. As before, do not move, and soon the bird will be drinking the syrup without fear. After he leaves, rest up a little, then move the cup from its support. Hold it in the same position it held before you moved it. Stay perfectly still, and when the bird comes back he will drink while you hold the cup for him.

All this takes a lot of patience, but if you want to

hand-tame free, wild birds, you will find it well worth the trouble. Do not try to rush it or you will fail.

You now have a hand-tamed ruby-throat. If you would like him a little tamer, it will not take long.

Hold the feeder as before, and when he comes, gently, and very slowly, start moving the feeder from side to side, as if a breeze were moving it. Move the cup this way only an inch or two on the first visit. The next time he comes, move it about four inches. If you have been sitting, you now stand, and when he comes again, you wait until he is taking a good drink, then, with the cup swaying gently, you walk very slowly along. You must do this just about as slowly as you can go for the first few times, then you can gradually increase your speed to a moderately slow but very smooth walk. The bird will stay with you for ten or fifteen steps.

Do not be satisfied with only one tame humming-bird, tame all you can. These birds, like all other creatures, have their tragedies, and many of them die.

Little Peter Honey, my neighbor's boy, kept some rabbits in the barn. A hummingbird had twice whizzed past his head on her way out of the building when he was going in to feed them. He thought perhaps she had built her nest in the barn. When he had not seen her for almost a week, he felt pretty sure she was sitting on eggs.

Peter climbed up into the hay loft and found the little bird, but she was in the center of a large spiderweb that was spun across the window in the back side of the barn. She was dead and tied up like a big fly. Peter brought her over to me. The tiny bird was stiff and dry, thoroughly dehydrated and mummified.

I asked Peter if the spider was still there. He took me up in the hay loft, and the spider was busy repair-

**76**

ing her web. We watched her finish the job, then Peter tossed a big grasshopper into it, and when the spider grabbed the insect, I grabbed her.

I mounted the spider and hummingbird in plastic cases and sent them to a friend of mine.

I was never much interested in spiders, and about the only thing I ever read about them was a long time ago; it had to do with the one who scared the daylights out of poor little Miss Muffet.

Some readers might like to know the name of the spider who killed the ruby-throat, but all I can say is that it was a big gray barn spider. I asked my entomologist friends, George McGinley and John Dimond about it, but I could not give them a good description. I started kidding them, but they both jumped on me with bird questions: "It is a big white bird; what is its name? Is it a whooping crane, a trumpter swan, a white heron, a mute swan, a white ibis?" I guess we will have to settle for a big gray barn spider!

Hummingbirds often get trapped in buildings, especially those with screened porches which are not equipped with strong springs. By telling you the following incident, I may save the lives of many of these birds.

A pretty little girl named Viola lived at Camp Norman on the banks of the Charles River in Millis, Massachusetts. She loved all wild creatures and would sit for hours waiting for the hummingbirds to come and drink from a feeder held in her hands. Her birds were very tame, and sometimes when Viola had forgotten to fill the feeders and the screen door was open, they would fly onto the porch looking for syrup. Occasionally, in the morning, one of Viola's family would find a hummingbird who had spent the night inside the porch.

One time the family went away for a few days, and no one remembered to shut the screen door. A hummingbird had gone inside the porch, the wind had blown the door shut, and the poor little thing was a prisoner. Fortunately, a friend of the family checked the camp to see if everything was all right and discovered him. He had been locked in for a long time and was weak from lack of nourishment, but he was lucky, for he was in the hands of a naturalist who knew how to take care of him. That was the last hummingbird to be trapped in the porch of the Norman, because Angus, who is Viola's father, put a very strong spring on the door and now it shuts tight.

On one occasion, I saw a hummingbird buzzing around some hollyhocks and noticed that one of his feet looked like a glob of used chewing gum. I watched him a few minutes and could see that he was having trouble with that foot, so I decided to help him out a little.

As soon as he left the hollyhocks, I picked off all the blossoms but one, and when the bird came back I had my hand wrapped around it. He buzzed around a bit, wondering what had happened to the other blossoms and then finally stuck his head in the one I was holding, and I quickly closed my hand.

The hummingbird did not struggle a bit as I took him from the blossom; he let me feel his foot and made no attempt to pull it away. It was all snarled up with thin blue silk thread. I very carefully cut the thread away and found that his middle toe was stiff and straight; there was nothing I could do about that, but perhaps he could. I took him out to the hollyhocks and opened my hand. He lay on his side for a few seconds, looked around, then rolled over to sit on my thumb while he picked and pulled on the stiff toe. He preened his feathers a little, then went to work on the toe again; he pulled so hard that he went over backwards and off my thumb, but was back on it immediately; then he got a good grip on it and buzzed his wings for a few seconds before he took off. The little bird showed no sign of fear while all this went on. I don't give a hoot what anyone else thinks, but I feel mighty sure that that bird knew exactly what I was going to do from the moment I took him in my hand.

It has always seemed strange to me that so many learned people will not believe that a bird can reason. Even some biologists will not believe it. Just recently a naturalist was lecturing a junior high class on wild birds. He told the students that birds cannot reason; that their actions are merely guided by trial and error. He did not tell them that trial and error are the very things that developed the brain of man and made him the intellectual superior of all living things. He did not realize that while he talked on, a boy in the class was wondering how it would be possible for a bird to be able to distinguish success from failure through trial and error, if that bird could not reason.

You may have heard that hummingbirds will sometimes travel south in the feathers of a wild goose. You have never heard of a hummingbird being seen actually getting on a goose to take the trip. Many of you have accepted the story as nothing but a fairy tale. Unless you were a wild goose or could talk to a goose, it would be difficult to prove.

One evening a friend called at my studio and laid a Canada goose on the table, then took a male ruby-throat hummingbird from his tobacco pouch and placed it on the head of the goose.

"Al," he said, "I shot this goose down on the Cape this morning, and when I picked him up, this little fellow

**79**

rolled out of his feathers. He was still alive but died in my hand."

I am just as sure that ruby-throat hummingbirds will ride a goose as I am that aviators ride planes.

# 11

The hairy woodpeckers who visit my feeder will take suet from my hand, but even long after they have been hand-tamed they will not come to the hand if they can get suet any other way.

Red-breasted nuthatches will take small pieces from the hand, once they are tamed, regardless of how much suet may be in the feeder, but not a woodpecker. He is not a bit afraid, apparently, but for some reason he will work his head almost off chipping away at frozen suet in preference to taking fresh bite-sizes from me.

**HAIRY WOOD-PECKER** *likes to play hide-and-seek.*

It took me a very long time to hand-tame my first hairy woodpecker. They were coming to my feeder for nine or ten years before one of them took suet from my hand. Perhaps this was because I spent most of my time on the easier species who came in flocks, birds like the grosbeaks, purple finches, and others who would come when called. Chipper, as the children named the hairy woodpecker I tamed, will pay no attention whatever to my call although he was tamed the same way as the other birds. His command words are: "Here, Chipper, here, Chipper!"

I could stand out in the yard with a chunk of suet in my hand and call Chipper all day long, and he would peck away at an apple tree a few yards away and pay no attention whatever.

For many years Chipper would pick away at the

suet while my hand rested against him. But if I *held* the piece of suet, with my hand blocking the suet hole, he would not touch the food; instead, he would set his shoulder against the edge of my hand and try to push it away from the hole so that he could get at the suet there.

I have tried to find the answer to this, and the only thing I've come up with is that Chipper is a gentleman and has no intention of stealing suet from me.

Perhaps because he feeds alone and usually takes his food from a hole where no other bird can even see it, he has never had a morsel of food stolen from him and has not acquired the habit of stealing that is seen among so many other species. All birds of other species who visit my feeder will snatch food from the bill of other birds every chance they get. Even a nuthatch, who is much like the woodpecker in feeding habits, will swoop down and snatch a sunflower seed from the mouth of another nuthatch — but not Chipper. After much training he will take suet from my fingers, but only when my hand is resting against the side of the house or the suet log. As long as the suet is resting against something that Chipper can *climb*, he will chip off a piece. Perhaps he thinks there is no difference between that and taking a piece from the suet hole.

Until I find a better answer, I will go along with that idea.

In the summer of 1960, a pair of hairy woodpeckers and two young ones came to my feeder every morning for a few weeks. Then the parent birds and one of the young stopped coming. I knew they were dead, because the young one remaining was not old enough yet to leave his parents. I could not suspect a hawk of taking three woodpeckers at one time, and I was beginning to wonder if there was something wrong with the suet I had fed them, but I checked it, and it appeared to be all right.

A month went by before I knew the fate of the hairy woodpeckers. They had been shot by a neighbor for digging their dinner out of a valuable ornamental shrub. They had already raised havoc with a fine hydrangea bush, and it was the birds or the shrubs.

All through the following winter I had only the one hairy woodpecker; and he grew to be the large, beautiful bird we named Chipper.

Early last fall I was stacking my winter supply of firewood in the ell, and Chipper flew in to take a look. He hopped around, poking his nose into every knothole and rotted part of the wood he could find, then he sailed over my head and flew up into the attic. I kept right on stacking up the wood, and every few minutes I could hear him chipping away at something up there. When I had finished my chore, I went up to see if I could steer him out through the ell door.

Chipper was hanging on the window screen, trying to peck his way out. The screen was nailed to the outside of the window sash, so I tried to steer Chipper down, but he could not get the idea. He flew around and around, chattering like a kingfisher. Finally he seemed to realize that if he wanted to get out, the only way he could do it was to let me carry him out. He settled on the window sash and did not move a muscle while I picked him up and carried him down to the yard.

He knew just what I was doing; his little tummy kept a normal beat, and when I opened my hand he flew to a nearby apple tree. As soon as I started pressing fresh suet into the suet feeder, he flew over.

Chipper is now very tame and will cling to the window beading of the kitchen and ask for suet if there is none in the feeder, but he still refuses to come when called and he will not take suet unless it is held against something he can hang onto. Chipper will sometimes play hide-and-seek with me. He will land on the log feeder with a thump, eat a little suet, then hop downwards and around to the back of the log. He will stay perfectly still for a few seconds, then start his hopping climb until he is on top of the log, poke his head over the top, and peek down at me. Then he will go around the log as if asking me to follow, and soon he will peek at me from another part.

One time, I could hear him going down the back of the log, and I figured he would poke his head around the left side near the bottom. I followed him down with my head and when he peeked around he looked right into my face. His bill was about eight inches away from my nose. He stared at me for a few seconds, then all the feathers stood up on his head, and he spread his shoulders at me, but he clung right there. I backed away and made a scratching noise with my nail as I ran my finger across to the other side of the log. I could hear Chipper going around the other side to meet me, and when he poked his head around we were both staring each other in the face about eight inches apart, as before. We were about to try again, when a neighbor's dog came tearing in, and Chipper flew off.

There is an old barn about a hundred yards north of my lot, and one day a sparrow hawk was sitting on the peak of the roof. I watched for a moment and another one lit on the barn. They were considering it as a likely place for their nest, but they did not know that in a few weeks the old building would be used by the village children as a

**84**

hide-out and sheriff's office for playing cowboys and cops and robbers, and for wrestling matches, boxing bouts, and romping in the hay. I decided to help the hawks out. I set up a nesting box, and soon the female was sitting on three eggs.

Less than a hundred yards away, a pair of hairy woodpeckers had their nest in an old tree, and both pairs watched one another across the little field. I have sat and watched them for hours, and they put on a great show. The little hawks were always trying to catch the woodpeckers, and the woodpeckers were always teasing the hawks into trying. One of the hawks would be resting on top of the nest box, and a hairy woodpecker would fly to the little apple tree in the field and do everything he could to attract the hawk's attention. He would call as loudly as he could, bang away at the tree trunk with his back to the hawk, and if the bird did not come right over, he would fly in a sweeping circle that would take him close to the hawk and back to the tree again. He would make believe he was busy digging a grub out of the tree so that the hawk would think he was not being watched; then the hawk would come at him fast, but just as he was about to grab him, the woodpecker would side-step quickly, and all the hawk would get was a beakful of air.

The hawk would settle on the top of the apple tree and look around to see where the woodpecker had gone, and the woodpecker would poke his head around the tree trunk and look at the hawk, then cling-hop his way around until he was in plain, open view. The hawk would come at him again, but all he would get was another beakful of air. This game would sometimes last for ten minutes on the same tree, and the hawk was always the one to quit first.

Sometimes the woodpecker would prefer a flying game. Each time the hawk came at him he would wait till he was almost on him, then instead of side-stepping to avoid him, he would drop under the hawk, and by the time the hawk had straightened out, the woodpecker would be in a nearby tree, his back in plain view, and call out taunts to the hawk: *"He, he, he, you can't catch me!"*

I have watched dozens of these games and have never seen a sparrow hawk catch a hairy woodpecker, but I presume he gets one on rare occasions; there is no such thing as a constant victor.

The sparrow hawk is the only hawk I have seen a woodpecker play with. When a sharp-shinned hawk shows up in my orchard, the hairy woodpecker keeps his little mouth shut, and he does not turn his back to this one! The sharp-shin is hardly any larger than the sparrow hawk, but the woodpecker never shows himself when he is around.

Hairy woodpeckers are expert in hiding and can cling absolutely motionless for a long time; you cannot even see that one is breathing.

One day while I sat on an old log with my deer rifle on my lap, I watched a woodpecker chiseling away on an old dead yellow birch tree. As I watched the chips fly, he suddenly pulled his head back and glanced to his left, then quickly flattened his throat against the tree and was as still as the tree itself.

A few seconds later, a beautiful gosh hawk settled on the broken top of the old birch. He was a fine specimen and looked a pretty shade of blue with the sunlight on him and a cottony white cloud for a background. He twisted his head from left to right, then shook himself. He pulled

**86**

his head down so that he appeared to have no neck, lifted one foot, and in a few seconds appeared to be sleeping.

I sat watching the deer trail for about ten minutes then looked up at the hawk again; he had not moved. I looked below him for the woodpecker; I had not seen him leave and knew he was still there. It was hard to see him at first, but once I got my eye on him I could even see the color on the back of his head that stood out like a tiny red dot. He was in exactly the same position and clung there motionless no more than ten feet below the hawk.

I turned my head slowly and watched the trail for another ten minutes, then reached for cigarettes, and as I did so the gosh hawk left the tree. I watched him for a few seconds then looked up at the woodpecker.

He stretched his neck, looked from left to right, and then went back to his wood chipping.

I did not keep accurate time, but that bird had clung motionless to the old birch tree for at least twenty minutes.

# 12

The cowbird is not an easy bird to tame. It seems a little strange to me that most of the wild birds who are called "friendly to man" are the hardest to tame.

**COWBIRD**
*enjoys eating from Dianne Musson's hand.*

Flocks of cowbirds will walk around a farmer's feet and show no fear of him whatever. The house sparrow will build her nest behind a picture in your home, if she has the chance. The chipping sparrow will build hers in a tree beside your house. The starling will build in the attic. The robin will build on the wall of your house, if she can find enough support to hold the nest. The song sparrow will build hers in the clipped hedge that borders your lawn. The Baltimore oriole will hang her nest in your shade elm tree. The bluebird will build in the hole of the apple tree close to your house.

I have spent countless hours trying to hand-tame all these birds and have succeeded only with the robin and the cowbird.

I was about fourteen when I first became interested in the cowbird. At that time, I was collecting eggs and abandoned nests of small birds. I would take only one egg of each specie, and later, when the breeding season was over, I would collect the nests.

The two summers I collected, I found many cowbird eggs among the others, but did not see a cowbird near a nest. Years later, I found a summer yellow warbler's nest with one egg in it. As I turned to leave, I saw a female cowbird fly from a branch not more than ten feet from the nest. I watched her, and she flew to another branch a few feet away and sat there watching me. I backed slowly away, but kept my eyes on her. I sat down to watch, hoping she would come to the nest. From where I sat I could see about half of it; the rest was hidden by a few leaves, but I could see all around it.

I watched for about fifteen minutes, during which time I did not look away once. Then I walked over to the nest to clip off the three leaves from in front of it. I took another peek into it and now there were two eggs; one of them was a cowbird's egg!

The only way the cowbird could have reached the nest without my seeing her was to start from in back of it and line up every leaf she came to, and keep in back of that so she remained out of sight — and she must have left the nest the same way.

This happened nearly fifty years ago, and since that time I have tried every summer to catch a cowbird on a nest, but I never have.

The female cowbird is just as cautious with her love affairs, and I have never seen her accept the advances of a male. The male does not seem to be a bit shy; he acts as if he would enjoy putting on an exhibition. I have watched the beginning of a great many cowbird love affairs. A group will be feeding, when suddenly a female will walk away from the flock. She does not go through cute little wing and tail tremors or utter sweet little love notes, she just walks away from the flock. She does not look back to see if a male has noticed her; she acts as if she did not care, but she is well aware that several birds are following her.

The males, as far as I have seen, do not fight for

her, but just follow along as close to her as they can get. Now, she flies a short distance and all the males go up with her; then she walks again, and they follow suit. This is repeated three or four times; then they all take to the air, the female leading and the males following close behind and trying to push each other out of the race as they go. The female leads them across the open field to the edge of the woods and out of sight.

A few years ago, I watched a pair of hooded warblers building their nest in a small, dense, wild rosebush. I visited this nest every day, and the same morning the first egg was laid, I found the female warbler under the nest with her throat torn out.

I wondered if a cowbird would lay an egg in the nest if I took the whole bush and wired it to another rosebush that I could watch from one of my windows.

I cut the bush close to the ground and carried it home. I wired the base of it to my old-fashioned rosebush. I had not touched or disturbed the nest or egg in the least, and when the wiring was finished, the whole thing looked as natural as could be. I was very pleased with the job and felt pretty sure I would get movies of a cowbird on that nest.

While I kept close watch from my window, a female cowbird settled on the rosebush. She crawled through the bush until she was about two feet from the nest. She sat like a statue for a few seconds, looking at it; then she backed out of there as fast as she could go and flew off. Before the day ended, three different cowbirds looked that nest over, and they all acted the same way. I don't know how they knew it was rigged up, but they certainly did. I have yet to catch a cowbird on a nest.

In the early spring I always have large flocks of cowbirds at my feeders; sometimes as many as a hundred.

Some of these visit the feeder throughout the summer. One year I had about a dozen females coming in every day, and I began to feel a little worried for the birds who nest around my house. I felt that by tolling in the cowbirds, I might lose a lot of songbirds. So, when the nesting season was well under way, I spent a few days locating the nests near-by, that is, within three hundred yards of my house.

I did not keep exact count of the nests I found, but there were at least twenty that contained eggs and not a single cowbird's among them. This is perhaps another example of Nature's regulations; maybe the cowbirds know that they should not clean out an entire section, but scatter their eggs. I wonder too if the three that looked over the rigged warbler's nest would have used it if the warblers had actually built it there. It is rather confusing. Perhaps the cowbirds could not understand how a wild rose could grow out of an old-fashioned rosebush and were wondering why the warbler built there. This sounds very far-fetched, but so do a lot of Nature's truths. I certainly cannot account for the fact that no cowbird's eggs were laid in the nests near my house.

As smart as the cowbird is, she does overplay her hand now and then. On several occasions I have found too many of her eggs in the same nest. I found one black-cheeked warbler's nest with *four* cowbird eggs in it. The nest of a black-cheek could not hold more than two cowbirds, and I doubt very much if the tiny warblers could gather enough food to raise more than one cowbird. Another time, I found a wood pewee's nest with three cowbird eggs in it. I watched this nest day after day, and although the three cowbird eggs hatched out, only one of the birds was raised.

92

For many years I had been unsuccessful in hand-taming the cowbird. I was fast asleep when I tamed my first one. I had been sitting on my kitchen steps with a handful of bird seed for over an hour, and about a dozen cowbirds were walking around my feet picking up seed. It was a nice sunny day, so I walked out on the grass and laid on my back to take a sun bath. My right hand was flat on the ground, palm up, with some seed on it. I do not know how long I had slept, but when I wakened I could feel something on my hand. I lay perfectly still, and out of the corner of my eye I could see that it was a male cowbird. I spoke softly to him and waited until he had eaten the last seed and flown off, before I got up very slowly and went into the house for another handful of seed.

In a few minutes after I lay down again the cowbird returned and fed from my hand. An hour later I was at it again, only this time I sat on the grass. The bird was a little nervous at first, but in a few minutes he was at my hand again. A few hours later I sat on the steps with my hand close to my hip, and the bird came up on the steps after it. Three days later, he was quite tame and would not hesitate to come to my hand. I was very pleased about it. All I needed now was a good bright day, and I would have movies of him feeding on my hand.

The next day some children came around with air rifles, and I never saw that tame cowbird again. This took place about three years ago, and though I put in a great many hours trying to hand-tame another cowbird it wasn't until recently that I succeeded.

Early last spring, we had a few days of mild weather. There was no snow on the ground, and several flocks of cowbirds came in to the feeder. I spent all the time I could getting as close to them as possible, and some of

**93**

them were taming up a little. Then we had a few inches of snow, and the cowbirds could find nothing to eat.

I waited for them to come in at dawn, then threw out a little seed — just enough to make them want more. The snow remained on the ground for a few days, and the cowbirds, now about thirty in all, stayed near the feeder from dawn to dusk. By now they would come and feed while my hand remained on the feeder, and before long they were eating out of my hand. I had spent, in short intervals, about an hour each day for two weeks before the first cowbird would fly to my hand in the open.

The same method as that used for the chickadee tamed the cowbird; as with all other birds, it takes slow motion and a lot of patience.

# 13

The evening grosbeak is one of the many birds I do not know; by that, I mean by close acquaintance. I have read all I could find about them, but still know very little.

Evening grosbeaks visit my feeders on and off through the year, but they never stay very long. They will fill up on sunflower seed, then take off and not show again for days, weeks, or months.

**EVENING GROSBEAK** *can crack sunflower seeds easily.*

Evening grosbeaks were not seen in this section during the summer until about 1956. If my memory is correct, the first nest to be built in Great Pond was in a tall white pine near the Aurora town line. I spent a little time watching the birds, but could not find the nest. I covered this section fairly well, looking and listening for other evening grosbeaks but found none.

I made notes of my experiences with these birds, at the time, but they have been lost, so I can only guess at when I saw the next mating pair. I believe it was during the summer of 1957.

In my back wood lot there are several giant old white pine trees. They are at least one hundred and fifty years old, and at one time were shade trees in the cow pasture that has since grown into forest. In one of these a pair of evening grosbeaks raised their family.

Early one morning while I sat on the edge of Alligator Road with my movie camera, an evening grosbeak flew from the large pine tree. I paid little attention to it at first, because my mind was set on getting pictures of a fox. Minutes later, the grosbeak returned, and her babies were shrilling for food. The tree was about a hundred yards from me so I walked slowly toward it. When I was about halfway there, the babies stopped clamoring. For at least fifteen minutes they kept quiet and there was no sign of their parents. I went back to the road to wait for the fox — and the young grosbeaks began asking loudly for food.

During the next hour or so, the male bird entered the tree at least a dozen times.

I started over toward the pine again, and the babies clammed up at my approach, as they had before. I sat about thirty feet from the tree this time and stayed for almost an hour, but saw and heard nothing of the grosbeaks.

The following day I searched the dense tree with a pair of seven-power glasses, but could see nothing. During about fifteen minutes of my listening and searching the babies kept quiet and the parents did not show themselves.

I would have liked to climb the tree but was afraid to, because the week before I had almost broken my neck when I fell out of an apple tree while taking movies of nesting kingbirds.

I started back to the house and was about fifty yards from the pine tree when the young birds started in again . . . I gave up.

A few days later the parent birds were in my yard feeding two babies. The young birds looked exactly like the female.

Since that time, evening grosbeaks have been here with young every summer, but I have never been able to find their nests. A great many times I have heard them at my feeder, but the instant I opened the door they would take off. Sometimes there were only four or five; other times, as many as twenty, and one day I counted thirty-two in one flock, the largest number I have ever seen.

For the past two winters there has been one male who for some reason prefers to be alone. He never joins up with any of the visiting flocks. This bird is a beautiful old fellow, with a little lighter coloring than the average. I have tried many times to get him on my hand. A few weeks ago, we had a heavy snow and the tree branches were cased in it; the sun melted it a little, then the temperature dropped and put a shell on the branches. This made it difficult for the grosbeak to get at the buds; he was hungry and came in with a small flock of cowbirds. I placed my hand on the feeder, with sunflower seeds a few inches from my fingers, and the old cock bird ate those seeds while my hand was there. A little later I heard him call. I took a handful of sunflower seed and rested my hand on the feeder. A chickadee lit on my thumb and took a seed. I kept perfectly still, and the chickadee took another. The grosbeak sat looking at the food, and the feathers on his head stood up like the crest of an angry kingbird. He wanted that seed badly, but he was afraid to chance it.

I gently opened my fingers to let the seed spill on the feeder, then very slowly backed away from him and stood in the doorway to watch. He went right after the food. Just then a big truck went by and scared him and the cowbirds who had been feeding on millet in the yard.

I got more sunflower seed and held it on the feeder again, and this time the grosbeak came cautiously to my hand and took one. After that he lost all fear; now he will fly right to my hand even when it is not on the feeder.

This is the only evening grosbeak I have had take food from my hand who was not afraid of the camera.

I have had very little experience with these birds, but they seem to be very gentle. One morning I was calling the grosbeak to my hand, and a male cowbird settled on it. A few seconds later the old grosbeak was also there, and the two fed together. The cowbird spread his wings and opened his beak at the other, but the old fellow paid no attention to him, and they both fed till my hand was empty.

As I watched these two birds I could understand why Nature had given the evening grosbeak such a gentle disposition. The cowbird has a large, powerful beak, but the grosbeak could cut him in half with that chopper of his.

# 14

Many swallow admirers have asked me if I knew any way they could get these beautiful birds to come to the hand. I have never hand-tamed a swallow, but have had a lot of fun with them.

Every normal summer about two hundred young swallows hatch out on my place. I have cliff, barn, and tree swallows, and the tree swallows are my favorites. They are tamer and more intelligent in their attitude toward man than the others.

**TREE SWALLOW** *having difficulty entering his nest with two feathers tied together.*

When you try to help a tree swallow, he knows what you are up to and will sit quietly and accept it. The barn and cliff swallows will dive at your head, snapping their little beaks and cursing you with everything they have. It makes no difference how well they know you, if you try to get within ten feet of their nest, they give you exactly the same reception they give a cat.

When the tree swallow gets to know you, he will allow you to stand close to the nest even while he feeds his babies.

One year we had a month of nasty weather, and the swallows could not find enough flies to feed their young. Every day cliff swallows would drop dead babies from their nests. One evening I picked up five from the ground. Barn swallows would carry their dead away, and drop them in the long grass in the orchard.

I tried to figure out a way to help these poor little things. I cut some very thin strips of deer steak, dried them a little, then ground them up into pieces a little smaller than the head of a wooden match. Out in back of the barn I began flicking these little pieces of meat into the air. It was no use: the cliff swallows would not take them, the barn swallows would not take them, neither would the tree swallows.

I put up a rough shelf a few feet below the cliff swallows' nests and sprinkled dry flies (fish food) on the shelf, but they would not touch them. I finally decided that if a swallow would not feed dead flies to starving babies I could never hand-tame one. They probably would have taken a live fly, but if I could get one live fly, the swallow could get a hundred.

Barn and tree swallows will take feathers from the fingers of your upraised hand if they cannot find all they need to line their nest. They prefer the lower breast feathers of a white fowl, but will take other colors if they cannot get white ones. Chickens are scarce here in the village, and as far as I know there is not a single white one.

During our hunting season I always save the lower breast feathers of a ruffed grouse. They have a lot of white on them, and the swallows will take them almost as readily as the pure white ones. The children about have a great time with them on a breezy day when the swallows start lining their nests.

The kids will get up on the highest place they can find, and when they see a swallow coming their way, they toss up a feather. The bird swoops down and picks it out of the air. If they see more than one swallow coming, the children make bets. Each child picks out a bird and watches him carefully; there are cheers and boos as the winner goes off with the feather.

**100**

A breezy day is also best for getting a swallow to take a feather from your hand, because the movement of the feather will attract him. All you have to do is to take a large feather between your thumb and index finger, hold your hand straight up over your head, and stand still in an open place. The first swallow that comes along will take it if he needs it. This will happen so fast you may not even feel the quill of the feather leave your hand; you may not know the swallow has the feather until you see him in the distance with it in his bill.

A tree swallow can go into his nest box with a feather at such great speed that it is hard to get pictures of it without a fast camera. I already had several pictures of this action, but they were poor. I wanted to get some movies of it, so I took the two largest, widest white feathers I could find, and tied the quills together. The bird took them, and their large size slowed him down; when he tried to get through the small hole in the nest box, the feathers spread out across the entrance and he had to push a few times to get them in. I got a very nice run of film.

The closest I ever came to hand-feeding a swallow was the time I found a young tree swallow in the middle of my drive. I picked him up and carried him over to a syringa bush near the nest he had just left and sat him on a dead twig of the bush. It took him a minute to figure out what he was supposed to do. He clung to the twig with one foot and my index finger with the other, and while he was in that position the mother flew in and dropped a fly in his mouth.

The mother swallow had watched me pick him up while she sat on the top of the nest box. She was not the least disturbed, she knew just what I was going to do. She had seen me do the same thing before for one of her young. In fact, it was the mother bird who drew my attention to the baby in the drive; she kept circling around it, then flying to settle on the very dead twig I sat him on. I feel sure she was either telling her baby to try and fly to the twig, or asking me to put him there.

You cannot do this sort of thing for a barn or cliff swallow without having the whole bunch of them screaming and diving at you.

# 15

The story of Poe the Raven has little to do with hand-taming wild birds. She is the most intelligent bird I have ever known. Poe is so well known throughout the country that you may have met her yourself, and for this reason I am sure the first few months of her life will interest you.

**POE, THE RAVEN** *enjoys a swig from Walter Morrill's bottle. Walter visits Poe often. She knows the sound of his car a mile away and often flies to meet him.*

Poe is the pal and playmate of the Boy Scouts at Roosevelt Camp. She is a very famous little brunette and has been photographed by hundreds of people.

She was born on the side of a steep rocky ledge that was almost perpendicular, a solid wall of smooth rock. Halfway up this wall, a small cave cut in about four feet, and on the floor of this little hollow was the raven's nest. Ravens have raised babies in this spot as far back as our oldest resident's grandfather could remember, and most likely for thousands of years before that. Year after year, many have tried to reach the nest without success. It seemed impossible without wings. Finally some local trappers got their heads together and came up with the answer.

These three men were real trappers, they made their living at it and knew their stuff. They were brothers, Pete, Art, and Bob Larson. They tied two long ladders together end to end, leaving a few feet of play in between. A long rope was tied to the top of one ladder and a shorter rope was tied to the bottom of the other; then they were ready for the ravens.

**103**

The method of operation was to be as follows: Art would steady the ladders by holding the rope with the help of a tree on top of the cliff; Bob would get the ladders swinging with the bottom rope, and Pete would cling to the rope between the ladders and reach in and grab a raven on the rebound.

Art slowly let the ladders down the face of the cliff, and when Bob called out that the space between the ladders was in front of the cave, Art found his rope was not long enough to hitch around the nearest tree. They looked for a support, but there was none that would do without spending too much time on it. It would take too long to get back to camp and return with more rope, so Pete asked Art if he could handle it with his own power. Art said he could, and that was that.

A few inches of hard earth covered the top of the cliff, and Art cut a hole in the earth that he could hook his toes into; then they were ready for the job.

Art hung over the cliff straining on his rope; Bob was on the ground pulling on his; and Pete was being bounced around in the middle. After two tries, Pete could see that he would never get a raven unless he changed his position. He was missing the birds by about two inches; they had squeezed as far back in the cave as they could get. Pete figured that if he could get the right hold on the rope he could hang on with his left hand and by going in sideways he would have the full sweep of his right arm and shoulder, but it was difficult to get a good footing.

He twisted the rope around one leg and was ready. Bob pulled on his rope, and Pete thought his leg was coming off, but he stayed with it and on the rebound this time he got his raven. Then trouble broke loose. The raven screamed at the top of his lungs, beat his wings and smacked

**104**

Pete across his ear so hard it made him hear bells. Pete let out a yell. The other three baby ravens were screaming and banging about; Art and Bob were roaring with laughter; the parent ravens were diving and screeching over the cliff. Pete, holding the thrashing, screaming baby, was wondering what to do. He could not put the bird in his pocket, it was almost twice the size of a crow. He did not want to drop the raven down to Bob for fear of hurting it. Bob could not come up after it, because Art could not hold the weight of both men.

Art and Bob stopped laughing; the babies in the nest had stopped screaming, and the bird in Pete's hand was hanging like a wet, black rag. Pete was grinning now; he pulled himself close enough to the rope to hold it with three fingers and unbutton his shirt with his left thumb and index finger. After a little struggle, he got the raven inside his shirt and buttoned it up.

He went down the ladder, and Bob put the bird in his shirt. Pete went up again and got another baby. This time it was easy. The birds were quiet, and Pete got one on the first swing. His shirt was already open and this bird did not thrash as much as the first one had.

I now had a baby raven to tame. Feeding her was no problem; she was old enough to eat anything from steak to milksop. She was a very large bird, even for a raven, and in a few days would be able to fly.

I put her in a large cage that was built on the side of the barn, and in three days she had her first flying lesson. Two of the Musson children, Jody and Dianne, both too young to go to school, were in the yard when I took Poe from the cage.

Poe fell in love with the kids at first sight; she went hopping right over to them and wanted to play. She hopped around their feet, flapping her wings and looking up at their faces. Jody and Dianne were delighted and began hopping around with her. Then Poe noticed Dianne's shoestring that had become untied. She grabbed the string and backed away with it, pulling as hard as she could. Dianne tied the string, and Poe grabbed it again and untied it. She went over to Jody and untied one of her shoestrings, and from that time on, Poe went after any shoestring she saw.

Poe soon learned to fly, and she was never caged again while I owned her. She never came to the window to ask for food as the other birds did, but if I opened the door, she would be on the steps before I could get there.

She was very jealous of the children and would not let any other raven or crow, or other large bird, come near the place. Sometimes we would hear a raven or crow off in the distance, and Poe would already be way up in the sky circling over the house to guard her little friends. As soon as she spotted the other bird, she would go right after it; we would hear their battle cries, and Poe would soon drop like a rock from the sky. She would always land right at the children's feet and look up at them as if to say: "Don't be afraid, kids, Poe will watch over you!"

One day while Jody and Dianne were playing in the yard, a big brown bird dog came trotting up the drive to play with them. The dog's name was Silver; he loved the children as much as Poe did, but the raven had never seen him before so knew nothing of this. Poe was sitting on the peak of the barn sunning herself and half asleep when Silver let out a gleeful bark and pranced around the children. Poe left the barn like an arrow and went straight at Silver, smacked him a wicked blow on the back of his head, and knocked the big dog right off his feet. Poor Silver did not know what had struck him. When he saw Poe coming down at him again, he let out a yell and started out along the driveway as fast as his legs would carry him, but he was not as fast as Poe. She smacked him another blow between his ears and chased him right up to the house he lived in, and Silver yelped all the way.

Silver did not come near the house for a week; then he got up enough courage to come halfway up the drive. He stood still and watched Poe playing with the children. The raven spotted him and hopped a few feet toward him with her shoulders spread, and Silver lowered his head, put down his tail, turned around, and slowly trotted back.

Poe was very fond of her bath and would sometimes ask for her washbowl three or four times a day, and she always got it. One day while she was splashing about in her bowl, Silver came cautiously up the drive, and one of the children put a dish of table scraps on the ground for him. He very slowly approached the food, but never took his eyes off Poe. One of the children was stroking his back while he ate the scraps. Poe spotted him. She hopped out of the dish, shook herself vigorously, then sat watching the dog. Silver backed away a few feet from the food, and they both sat watching each other. Poe shook herself again, and started hopping toward the dish of scraps. Silver backed off a few more feet. The bird picked out a piece of baked potato skin and hopped off to one side with it. Silver's eyes never left her as he walked slowly to the scraps and finished them. After that they were friends. They often ate from the same dish, but Silver always let Poe eat first.

**107**

Whenever I left the house on foot to go fishing, I always looked around for Poe and tried to sneak off without her seeing me, but I was seldom successful.

One morning I went to King Pond, which is a little more than a mile hike from my house. At this time, if you were lucky, you could take some nice salmon and trout from this little pond. I had just made my first cast when I heard a raven call. I looked out across the pond and saw a tiny black speck heading my way; it was coming fast and flying high. I waved my hand and it kept coming, so I knew it was Poe. In a few seconds she was circling over my head, then she closed her wings, dropped like a rock, and landed on my head, screaming as loud as she could.

Poe often went fishing with me; she loved it. Sometimes when I walked a fairly smooth road she would fly down and hop along by my side. If I had to cut through woods she would circle over my head and keep me in view. If I walked a fairly wide road, she would fly slowly along with me, the tip of one wing a few inches from my face.

Poe was sitting on an old log watching every cast I made, until I got my first strike. She left that log like a retriever going after a duck. She danced around the edge of the water, and I knew the fish I had caught was not a salmon or trout. I reeled it in; it was a small chub. I tossed it up in the air and when it came down it went down Poe's throat without a hitch. She was a great catcher; she never missed.

The next two fish were trout, the same size as the chub, but Poe sat on the log. The third fish was another chub, and she knew it the instant the fish struck, for she was dancing around again with her big mouth wide open. I never gave Poe a trout, and somehow she always knew

**108**

what I had hooked before I did. She knew that only the trash fish were for her, and she showed no interest at all when a trout or salmon was on the line. I don't know how Poe could tell, but she could and never was wrong. Perhaps she could see the fish in the water.

My friend Bill Butler and Poe were great friends. She followed him around like a dog and was always with him every time he stepped into the yard.

Bill was building a boat in my barn, and of course, Poe was right there too. Bill was keeping the boat as clean as he could because he wanted to keep the natural wood finish. Poe had been sitting on the gunwale watching Bill put in the middle seat when she very impolitely turned her back to him and dropped half a cup of second-hand blueberries smack on the floor of the boat. Bill quickly wiped it off, then slowly sweeping his hand in a half-circle over Poe's head he said: "You turn around when you do that; understand?"

Poe's feathers stood up on her head, and she cocked it to one side as Bill went through the command again. She did understand. A little later Poe, still on the gunwale, dropped her next card on the floor of the barn and never soiled the boat again, although she stayed with Bill for the following week till he finished it. Poe was only three months old at the time, but had understood what was expected of her on just two commands.

When the boat was ready for the finish, Bill laid a varnish folder and a pencil on the seat and Poe instantly grabbed them and flew to a high beam of the barn. Bill yelled at her to bring them back, and she instantly dropped them in the boat. He picked up a sliver of wood about the same size as the pencil, then the envelop the varnish folder came in, and handed them to Poe. "These are yours, but leave mine alone," he said. "Understand?"

Poe took the stick and envelope and played with them for days, but she never touched the folder or pencil again.

Tame ravens love the company of people and if left alone with no one in sight they will go searching for someone to talk to and play with. It makes no difference if the person is a total stranger, all the raven wants is a little attention from a human being.

If you give a tame raven his freedom, be sure to cage him every time you leave your place, if only for a few hours, or you will find yourself in trouble. As intelligent as the raven is, he never learns to keep his sharp powerful talons out of tender human flesh, and when he settles on a stranger's shoulder he will draw blood.

One day I was very busy on some taxidermy, and not wishing to be disturbed, I locked up the house and took my work to an upstairs room. The specimen I was working on was in poor condition, and six hours passed before I came downstairs. I went out to see if Poe needed anything, but she was not around. The children were all away on a picnic, and this section of the village was like a ghost town.

A phone call came in a little while later, from some people up over the hill, asking me to get my raven; she was trying to carry off a visitor's baby and the child's mother was almost scared to death.

I went up right away. Poe was sitting on the peak of the house looking down at the poor lady, who was too scared to move and stood holding the baby close to her breast.

I apologized to her and tried to explain that Poe loved children and only wanted to play, but she thought

**110**

Poe's neck should be wrung right then and there. I promised her Poe would never bother her again, called the raven down, and took her home. There was nothing else to do.

It would be cruel to deprive Poe of her freedom, and I had to find a home for her where she would not be lonesome. The Roosevelt Scout Camp in the wilderness was the place for Poe. Soon she had all those fine youngsters to play with.

A few years later, poor Poe found herself left alone again. Even the caretaker of the camp had gone away. Poe could stand it no longer, so she went up in the air, higher and higher, until she spied a group of people bathing on a lake. Down she went, down, down, down, screaming with joy as she landed on the bare shoulders of a swimmer. The poor fellow was almost frightened to death. He had no idea what struck him; he saw a great black thing above his head and before he had time to think, Poe's sharp talons were digging into his flesh. A man rushed out of a camp with a rifle and was about to shoot the raven, when someone cried: "Don't shoot; it's a Scout. It's Poe!"

The man who had saved Poe's life called her over and took her back to the scout camp.

After that, one of Poe's wings had to be clipped to protect the public. I have not seen her for five years, but I hear she seems to be quite happy, has all the company she needs, and meets thousands of people at sportsmen's shows and other events. I still miss her very much.

# 16

The cedar waxwing pictured here was not hand-tamed at the feeder, but because so many bird lovers have asked if the waxwing could be hand-tamed, I thought his story might be of interest.

Some people have reported cedar waxwings in Maine during the snowy weather, but I have never seen one here after the middle of November. If they came here in the winter, I believe I could hand-tame them in a week with dried currants.

**CEDAR WAXWING**
*This specie loves blueberries and other small fruits, and also eats the bugs found on them.*

Some who read this book may have nesting waxwings on their property, and if they would like to hand-tame one they could go about it the same way I did.

Waxwings can be tolled to nesting places much the same as other birds are tolled to the feeder. If plenty of nesting material is placed out in an orchard, a flock of these birds will stay around to build. If the same flock should arrive at the orchard and find no suitable building material they might move on.

I do not mean that you have to have an orchard to attract waxwings, because these birds will build in almost any kind of tree, but they do seem to prefer apple trees. I have seen them build in fir, spruce, pine, larch, maple, oak, beech, hemlock, cedar, birch, and lilac, and at elevations from four to fifty feet above the ground. But in one nesting season I located eleven waxwing nests on and near my place, and nine of them were in apple trees; three in my orchard.

This is not because we have an abundance of apple trees, there are thousands of other kinds to every apple tree.

The first two years I lived here in Great Pond I would sit on the steps and watch flock after flock of waxwings settle in the apple trees, stay a few minutes, and then continue on their way north. I did not have a single nesting pair on my place until I put out materials for them.

Nesting or building material should be hung up before the waxwings arrive, otherwise they may keep going. They will take any kind of string or thread except sewing cotton. Thin thread should never be used, and pieces longer than four inches of any material should also be avoided.

Most birds seem to prefer burlap. I cut a burlap bag into four-inch squares and unravel them. I tie a dozen or more of these strands in the center, then tie the bundle in a tree or shrub where the birds can see it from a good distance. I put out about a dozen of these bundles in as many different places around my house, and all of them where I can see them from a window. Just as soon as one bundle has been taken I put another one in its place and keep this up until the birds have all they need.

When a waxwing leaves with some burlap I watch her until she is out of sight, then I walk over to the spot where I last saw her, and wait for her to go over with more burlap. When she goes over I watch her again and keep this up until she leads me to her nest.

If you like taking pictures, the waxwing makes a beautiful subject, and for movies it is hard to beat a pair of the birds fluttering in the air while trying to loosen a strand from a bundle of burlap. Every time I hang out burlap, I make sure to have some of the bundles set up with a good background where they will be in good light most of the day.

**114**

I was lucky enough to have a pair of waxwings build in a lilac bush close to my house. The nest was about eight feet from the ground, and by sitting on a step ladder I could put my hand on it. Twice a day I would walk slowly around the lilac bush and speak to the birds. When the five eggs hatched, I increased my visits to four a day. The birds were used to seeing me near their nesting bush, so now I went up the ladder and sat watching the babies for a minute while the parents sat on a nearby spruce and watched me.

I went to the nest every two hours; the parents lost all fear of me, and when the babies opened their eyes the first thing they saw was my ugly map staring them in the face. They didn't know what they were looking at, but they did know it was nothing to fear, or their mother would have told them. I would place my hand on the edge of the nest, and the parents would stand on the other side and feed the babies.

They grew fast and soon were big enough to take blueberries. Sometimes a baby would be unable to pass a large, undigested berry and the mother bird would take care of that right away. The baby would back up to the edge of the nest, head down, little fanny as high in the air as it could get with its tail up over its back and feathers parted so that the mother could get a clear view of the troublesome berry that looked just like a blue eye. The mother bird would very gently take the berry and swallow it; then the baby would settle back in the nest.

Several cars came into my drive soon after the babies began eating berries. One car parked a few feet from the lilac bush; a group of fishermen got out, and it took them quite a long time to assemble their tackle, change from city to fishing clothes, and get their luggage together

**115**

for the long hike to Alligator Lake. All this activity had frightened the parent waxwings, and they had not fed their babies, who were hungry. I picked a few blueberries and took them up to the nest. Taking a berry between the tips of my thumb and index finger, I offered it to one of the babies, but he would not take it; so I tickled him under the chin with it until he opened his mouth and took it. Four of the babies took a berry, but one refused to have anything to do with me, and although I fed two or three berries to the babies every day after that until they left the nest, that one bird never took food from my hand.

When the babies first left the nest, they perched in the lilac bush for a day, and I would be feeding one bird while the parents fed the others a few feet away.

The babies now looked exactly like their parents except for little brown streaks on their breasts and the absence of the tiny red waxy appendages on their wings.

The waxwing pictured here is one of those babies, photographed a few days after he left the nest. He could fly, but was so tame he would let me take him from the bush and place him on a twig, and would take berries from a spray held in my hand, while I took movies of him.

If you have nesting waxwings you will most likely have trouble with jays. Blue jays do more damage to cedar waxwings than all the other predators put together. There is only one way to stop the jay and that is with a dose of lead. In the season of 1961, I had five nesting pairs of waxwings on my place; the nest and eggs of one pair were destroyed by a jay while I stood under the maple tree and yelled at her. The young of two other nests were taken by the same jay and its mate; then the jays tore down the nests of cliff swallows and snatched full-grown barn swallow babies as they left their nest. This one pair of jays was re-

**116**

sponsible for the lives of twenty birds in one week. I kept trying to scare them off, but the instant I went into the house they would be back again.

One morning I was watching a pair of barn swallows trying to get their baby off the ground for its first flying lesson, when one of the jays snatched him from the ground and carried him to an apple tree, and began tearing him apart — and that just about tore me apart. I knew it would not be long before the jays would get my waxwings in the lilac bush. I shot the jay.

I am well aware of "Nature's wonderful scheme." I realize also that the jay must eat and provide her family with food, but she is not going to feed my pets to her babies if I can prevent it.

Other creatures have to eat, too, the poor old man-eating tiger, the corn borer, the potato bug, the tomato-hawk, the moth caterpillar, the cabbage caterpillar, the mosquito, the black fly, the tapeworm, the louse, and the poor little germs that stretch us out on a hospital bed or carry us off to the Promised Land — all these are just as much a part of "Nature's wonderful scheme" as the individual predator who would clean out our pets. If we are going to go along with Nature's scheme, why not do it right? Why discriminate? If we allow a predator to kill our pets and do nothing about it, why should we allow our doctor to kill Nature's poor little germs when they attack us?

If a jay or any other predator makes a second trip to your feeders, and you have actually seen him kill a pet, it's up to you to get rid of him, because the responsibility is really yours.

The Canada jay is not classed in this book as a wild bird to be hand-tamed, for the simple reason that it does not have to be tamed to come and take food from the

**117**

hand. The Canada jay is just about the prize glutton of the bird world and unlike the blue jay, who carries off all the food he can find and then forgets where he puts it, he eats great quantities, then stuffs his throat and beak with all he can hold to carry off, and remembers where he hides it.

A Canada jay who has never seen a human before will not hesitate to fly to a lumberjack's hand and help him eat his lunch. The only fear the Canada jay shows is when he first feels the texture of human flesh under his feet, and in this all wild things are the same, whether it be a skunk, chipmunk, or chickadee.

The Canada jay is a very intelligent bird although he appears to show little fear of anything. Last winter, Ed Musson and Bill Butler were cutting logs well into the wilderness north of Great Pond Lake and when they stopped work for lunch they each had a Canada jay on their sandwich as soon as the wrapper was taken off. Ed had his movie camera close by and took pictures of a jay on his hand eating his sandwich and the jay paid not the least attention to the camera clicking away not more than a foot from his ears.

Last winter I saw the largest, most beautiful Canada jay I've ever seen clinging to the suet feeder. He was quite fearless. This bird was a large male and so rich in coloring that I decided to trap him and make a close study of him. I prepared a cage for him with gravel, water, fruit, seed, and suet. I had expected him to be very happy and to try to eat himself to death, but instead, the feathers on his head went straight up and he was mad clean through. He screamed and beat about so much I was afraid he would knock his brains out, so I put the cage outside and opened the door, and the bird flew to a nearby tree where he sat looking at me and cursing for all he was worth. This bird

**118**

visits the feeder occasionally and will come and feed within a foot of my hand, but he would starve to death before he would come any closer. He came again this fall and although three other jays fed from my hand the big male kept his distance while he kept up a continuous warning chatter. I don't know whether other Canada jays would act this way but I believe they would. This jay did not seem to be the least bit afraid; he was just good and mad.

There are, of course, many other kinds of birds you can experiment with along the same lines I did with cedar waxwings. Always try to be patient and allow the parent birds plenty of time to get used to seeing you before you even touch the nest. Robins are very easy to tame this way, and sometimes the parent bird will come looking for you and take raisins out of your hand to take to its young. The babies should be at least half grown before you offer them raisins.

A few years back, I watched a little boy taking worms from his bait can and dropping them into the mouths of four baby robins. The parent birds sat about ten feet from the nest and watched too. The boy asked me if there was any place handy he could dig some more worms. Behind my barn we found a few. We went back to the robins, and the boy stood with the can in his left hand while he fed a worm to a baby with his right hand. The mother robin flew to the can still in the boy's hand, and dug out a worm and fed it to another baby. The boy then set the can on the ground at his feet, and the mother robin cleaned it out.

I have hand-fed many species of birds in the field this way. I once kept a family of indigo buntings supplied with small caterpillars of the cabbage butterfly. The female would sit on my thumb while she took the caterpillars from

**119**

the palm of my hand and fed her young. The beautiful male was not so trusting and would come no closer than six feet from my hand, and all the time I was near the nest he kept up a steady *chip, chip, chip,* warning note.

# 17

If you are just starting in with birds
and would like to know more about
them, you should have a good bird
book or bird guide. Do not get a
cheap one. The cheap guides are very
poorly illustrated and will only con-
fuse you. If you cannot find a good
book, go to the nearest public library and the librarian will
be glad to help you. Do not believe everything you read
about birds in newspaper columns either. Some of these
columns are taken from good bird books and are wonderful, but a lot of them, especially in smaller papers, give daily
reports of birds seen at local feeders, and a great many of
these are wrong — cases of mistaken identity.

**PURE BLACK
ROBIN**
*Any bird may be
white, vari-colored,
or solid black like
this robin.*

A lady reported a male redpoll as a "red-breasted
song sparrow"; a man reported over a hundred different
species at his feeder at the same time. A male purple finch
with his crest up was reported as a "cedar waxwing"; a
male evening grosbeak as a "Baltimore oriole." Starlings,
grackles, and cowbirds have been reported as "blackbirds."
Reports such as these can be very misleading to a person
just starting in with birds.

Several years ago a newspaper came out with the
following: "Finches are very common birds and are found
in every country except Australia." The day this appeared
in the paper I had several Australian finches in my aviary.
I notified the newspaper office and was told that the error
would be corrected in the next issue. I was also told that it
was only a filler.

Sometimes, when a newspaper is late and the linotype operator has just cast his last slug, the make-up man finds he needs a few more lines to fill a blank space. There is no time to hunt up copy if the paper is to go out on time, so the lino operator is asked to set a few lines as fast as he can. The subject is of no importance, speed in setting type is; so the operator bangs out the first thing that enters his mind. These little items are seldom seen in modern papers. Now if they need a filler it will be: "Give to the Heart Fund"; or the March of Dimes, or some other worthy cause gets a little boost.

Some birds are very easy to identify; others not so easy, and some are extremely difficult.

Late last summer one of the children near-by pointed out an immature warbler to me and said: "Al, what kind of bird is that?"

I could see the bird fairly well, but could not be sure. I told the little boy it was a warbler.

"I know that, but what kind of a warbler?" he asked.

I told him I wasn't quite sure, but if the bird would only let out a few notes I could give him the name. The words were no sooner out of my mouth than the warbler let out a trill. The boy smiled and looked at me. I looked at the boy, but I did not smile. I still could not be sure.

"Gosh, Al," he said, "I thought you knew all the birds in the world, and you don't even know the name of that little warbler!"

I told him I had studied birds since I was his age, and if I could live until he was my age, I would *still* have a lot more to learn. He seemed satisfied, and so was I.

Size, body color, and the pattern of markings are the main keys to quick identification of birds at close range,

**122**

but are not wholly dependable. Many different species look much alike to the beginner. But if you watch birds very closely, you will notice that nearly every specie has a different way of moving on the ground and in the air.

If you listen carefully to birds you will find that although the notes of some species are somewhat like those of another, there is a marked difference once you get to know them. The robin sounds like a robin; the thrush sounds like a thrush; the purple finch like no other bird.

If you watch the way birds move on the ground, you will notice differences. A robin runs like a robin; a cowbird walks like a cowbird; a grackle walks like a grackle; a fox sparrow hops like a fox sparrow; and a junco hops like a junco.

It is the same with birds in flight. The flight habit of one specie may somewhat resemble that of another, but once you get to know them, there is enough difference in most of them to make correct identification.

The notes of some birds are difficult at first to pin down. The call of a male woodcock is often mistaken for that of a night hawk. The note of the redpoll sounds almost the same as that of a goldfinch. A male English house sparrow can sound very much like a male evening grosbeak. And I think the chickadee will really fool you for a few seconds when he calls like a phoebe.

If you have a pair of nesting starlings you will surely be fooled once in a while by the male as he serenades his mate. In my opinion, this bird is the greatest imitator of all, and an old, well-trained male starling will build up a greater vocabulary than a good black hill myna.

One day in the summer of 1961 when the lilacs were in full bloom, I went upstairs to lie down and read near the open window. I do this many times when the lilac and fragrant syringa are in bloom. A strong breeze was coming from the Union River Valley, and the scent of lilacs it brought me was mild enough to be very pleasant.

I lay in solid comfort reading F. Whitehouse Anderson's *Bushed.* I had read the book before — about a boy lost in the Maine woods — and I had enjoyed it so much I was reading it again.

There is a lot of difference in reading a book about the Maine woods in a stuffy kitchen and reading the same book near an open window with the smell of woods and lilac in your nostrils and the song of birds in your ears. As I read along I heard a black duck quack three times along with the notes of other birds. The sounds went along naturally in tune with the book, but the duck quacked again, and this time it sounded pretty close. I glanced toward the window and there was a starling. His imitation of the black duck would have fooled the best duck hunter in the country.

He flew to a nearby maple tree and went into full song. I made a list of his imitations on the inside cover of my book, and here it is: black duck, cat, robin, grey squirrel, sparrow hawk, wolf whistle, bluebird, white-throat sparrow, blue jay, bobwhite, loon, white-breasted nuthatch, crow, chickadee, red-winged blackbird, dog, red squirrel. There were also other notes and warbles I did not recognize. Harsh notes like those heard on any city street were also included in the song. If I were a better naturalist, this list would contain at least a dozen more imitations, but there are many birds I know nothing about, and I could not very well give names to calls I did not recognize.

Some starlings move about more than others. The more a starling travels, the more he learns. A starling who never leaves a coastal town of eastern Maine will imi-

**124**

tate a gull, the whistle of a goldeneye duck's wings, the call of a tern, the sound of lobster pots being tossed into a boat, etc., etc., but he will rarely imitate the call of a bobwhite, because there are few of these quail in eastern Maine.

You may be walking along some day and hear someone call your name, or make some other remark. You stop and look around but see no one. You continue on your way wondering how you could have imagined it. You distinctly heard the voice. Later, as you pass the same place, you hear a wolf whistle, so you continue on your way without giving that smart aleck the satisfaction of looking around again. If you had stopped and looked the rooftops over carefully, you would have seen a starling. This has happened to hundreds of people, and very few of them have ever known that the voice belonged to a starling. I recall one incident that happened to me in Connecticut several years ago.

One day while I was visiting a naturalist friend who was chief taxidermist at the Museum of Science in Boston, Massachusetts, our conversation drifted to off-colored birds. John showed me the skins of several ruffed grouse he had collected in Connecticut. Some were a bright brick-red; the others were varying shades of blue-grey. John told me that the red grouse were taken on tobacco farms, and he was about to tell me where the blue ones were taken when he was called to the office. I waited in his studio a few minutes, then left.

The following morning I was on a train bound for Connecticut. I wanted to get some pictures of the colored grouse in their natural habitat. I spent several days searching for the birds. I failed to find them; but I did enjoy myself.

**125**

One evening, after a wonderful dinner, I sat on the front steps of the old farmhouse where I was staying, and watched a Baltimore oriole in an elm tree. A voice called out "Dinner's ready, dinner's ready." The words were as well spoken as by any human voice, but I had already eaten dinner and knew it was a starling. If I had been waiting for a call to dinner, I would have been completely fooled.

At breakfast the next morning my hostess, Mrs. Birkbeck, told me the bird was eight years old and had picked up the call from her when she called her husband in to dinner. The starling could also say: "Get out of there, get out of there," and could swear just as well as her husband — and according to Mrs. Birkbeck, her husband was an expert in the gentle art.

Although the starling is considered an undesirable pest, he does have his good points. Years back, in horse and buggy days, the starling could feed on secondhand oats, and garbage was easily found. Now, with very few horses, daily garbage removal, garbage dumps kept burning, the starling has to work for his food and is fast becoming a valuable insect destroyer. He has wonderful eyesight, is quick as a flash, and never misses the tiniest insect he goes after. He will also eat many of the larger insects that other insectivorous birds pass up.

Ed Musson and I watched a hatch of some kind of flying ants leave the ground and go straight up in the air like a lot of tiny helicopters. A flock of seven starlings were perched on the roof of the old church about a hundred yards from the ants that were now about fifty feet in the air. The starlings spotted them and they all came over together. They circled, dove, and went up after the ants, cleaning

**126**

them up right and left. They followed them along with the breeze for about fifty yards, then as if obeying a command, they all swung around together and flew back to the church to wait for another hatch.

In a few minutes, the next hatch left the ground, and the starlings came at them again. This time I singled out a bird and counted his dips, dives, and twists, and when the starlings returned to the church my count was twenty-seven. One starling had destroyed twenty-seven flying ants in a few minutes.

It would be safe to say that between three hundred and fifty to four hundred ants had been taken on those two feedings by seven starlings. I would have liked to check on a few more hatches, but the trout were slowing up, and I wanted to get my choppers into a few more before they stopped biting.

Starlings have caused a lot of trouble, but so have termites. I feel that the starling should be protected as a valuable insectivorous bird.

A pet starling once won the honor of being judged "best bird in the show" at a National Bird Show in Boston, and a bird really has to be something special to win any prize at one of these.

Getting back to bird identifications again, I think some of the off-colored birds should be mentioned. Off-colored birds are often mistaken for another specie and sometimes, unless you are very close to the bird, it is easy to make this mistake.

Odd coloring in birds is fairly common, especially in young ones, but most of these moult out into normal color. I have seen a great many off-colored birds, sometimes referred to as "sport models," but I mention only those I have seen in the past twelve years here in Great Pond:

**127**

male English sparrow with white back
pure black robin
pure white cliff swallow
red-winged blackbird with white shoulder
    patch and two heavy white bars in each
    wing and the top of his tail white
grackle with white tail and wings
grackle with tail all white
robin almost pure white
slate junco with pale yellow crown
ruby-throat hummingbird with solid black
    back
cowbird with pale cream feathers
a bald eagle that was almost pure white

All these birds were seen on or near my feeders except the eagle, who fished at Great Pond Lake, a mile from my house.

You may find some of your off-colored birds a little hard to pin down. A white tree swallow is hard to tell from a white cliff swallow unless you know both very well.

One day Bob Larson, State Biologists Sid Howe and Bill Peppard and I were out on Great Pond Lake and just passing Turtle Rock when Bill pointed high over the treetops to the northwest. I glanced up and saw a large whitish bird coming in motionless, like a plane.

"It's an eagle, all right, but not Whitey," I told him. "It's not white enough for him."

Just then the bird moved his wings, and before I had a chance to speak, Bill said: "That's an osprey."

He was right. I had noticed that too, the instant the bird moved his wings. The osprey has a faster wing-beat, and his wings are more pointed at the tips than those of the eagle. Sometimes it's hard to tell what a bird is when it is motionless.

Bill knew about the white cliff swallow I had identified. He also knew I had seen the bird leave the mud nest, and that was identification enough, but like all top biologists, he was thorough.

"About that white swallow, Al," he said. "Why a cliff and not a tree swallow?"

I described the stockier look of the cliff swallow: his wings are broader and his notes are harsh squeaks and crackles. The notes of the tree swallow are sweet and musical like the notes of some of our warblers. Bill was completely satisfied.

He was testing me for the little but very important things so helpful in naming a flying bird, and if I had not known the very slight difference in the anatomy and feathering and voices of both birds I could not have given him a satisfactory answer.

Some day you may see a bird at your feeder that you cannot name and will not find in your bird guide. Foreign birds are often seen in this country.

Don't be too surprised if you see a flock of parakeets at your feeder some morning. Every year, thousands of imported foreign birds, animals, and reptiles are bought by the American people for pets. Quite often the pet owner becomes tired of his pet or finds that he has not the time to care for it. He first tries to sell it, then he tries to give it away, but nobody wants it. He thinks about taking it to the Animal Rescue people, then decides against it because he thinks the pet may be "humanely disposed of." He does not want his pet put to sleep, so he finally comes up with the bright idea of giving it "its liberty." He takes the pet out into the country and lets him go. Now he feels better; he

**129**

hasn't hurt the poor little thing, and it will be happy in the beautiful woods. He does not realize that he has unintentionally subjected his pet to almost sure death from slow starvation or violent death when a predator sees him.

Coyote pups, baby alligators, hamsters, parakeets, many species of foreign finches, Japanese robins, coatismundi, ocelots, and even a young Mexican burro have all been found in the New England woods. We do have occasional visitors direct from foreign lands — a finch or other bird now and then — but most of the foreign birds and animals in our woods were either abandoned by or escaped from their owners. Even experts find it hard to identify natural hybrids. Hybrids in finches are not common, but they do occur. Crosses in wild ducks are not uncommon; I believe about five per cent of our wild ducks are hybrids. I base this figure solely on what I have seen in the field and the hybrid specimens I have mounted over a period of almost fifty years.

Soon after the end of World War I, I was planning a trip to Europe. I had many canaries and foreign finches in my aviary that I had to unload before I could leave on the trip that would take at least a year. I soon placed the canaries and all the finches except three male Mexican redheaded linnets. Nobody wanted them because they are troublemakers in an aviary and have a nasty habit of scalping any bird they fight with.

Soon the day for me to leave came around. I sat looking at the Mexican linnets wondering what I could do with them. A large flock of purple finches were at the feeder, and I thought that because the Mexicans and purples were so closely related, they might get along together. I had just ten minutes to make up my mind. I opened a window and let the linnets out; they immediately

**130**

joined the purples and fed right along with them. I watched them for a few minutes and neither specie showed any sign of battle. In a few minutes I was on my way to the boat.

Thirteen months passed before I returned home. My mother had kept the feeder supplied during my absence, and she was telling me all about the bird visitors she'd had. The Mexican linnets had stayed with the purple finches and had left with them in the fall. They had returned with them in the early spring and had left again a few weeks before I got home.

The following late summer only two of the Mexican birds came in with the purple finches, but there were four hybrids with them. The feeder was close to a window and it was easy to pick them out. They were not so chunky as the purples, and their legs and tails were longer.

The following fall about twenty birds came in one flock, and one half of them were second cross or hybrids. The Mexican birds did not return.

That winter, we moved away from that section and I do not know what happened to the hybrids, but I suppose the Mexican blood gradually petered out, as is usually the case in such matings, until the pure strain of the majority showed again.

In the early spring of 1959, I was taking movies of redpolls feeding in my yard, when a larger bird dropped in to feed with them. I took the camera from my eye for a better look and was very much surprised to find myself looking at a beautiful male chaffinch. I could hardly believe my eyes and was so excited that I did the worst possible thing. I walked briskly toward the bird to make him fly so I could be absolutely sure he was a chaffinch. The redpolls were very tame and remained feeding, but the strange bird went through the air in half-circle swoops as if he were going to make a complete somersault then suddenly changed his mind. I was sure then. The chaffinch settled on a wild cherry tree and called three times — a bell-like *chink, chink, plink* — then went out of sight, and I never saw him again.

If I had only been a little more patient, the chaffinch would have stayed with the redpolls; I would have had nice movies of him and he would most likely have fed from my hand in time.

A lone chaffinch was later sighted in another section of Maine; it may have been the same bird.

Do not get discouraged if you have a little trouble in identifying birds at first. Bird study is not easy. In my younger days I have spent weeks and months trying to solve a bird problem and sometimes had to give up. Now, when I get stuck, I get in touch with our local game warden or our state biologists, or the University of Maine.

# 18

Nearly all my bird-loving friends are also camera fans. You probably are too, and I believe you would be interested in some of my camera experience in the wilderness.

I know very little about photography, but in the past five years I have filmed a great many species of wild birds and animals here in the Maine woods.

When I first tried to get close movies of birds I thought it was going to be impossible; they were afraid of the sunlight reflecting from the camera and would not come near it. I pasted strips of tape on the finish, but still the birds feared it. I finally found the answer entirely by accident.

At this time, I was working on the painting I have mentioned before, of two deer in the early morning mist. Every time I heard birds coming into the feeder I would go out with the camera and try again. Finally I gave up. I put the camera on the feeding platform while I rolled a cigarette. I smoked a while, then went into the house and got going on my misty problem.

About three hours later, one of the Musson children came in with my mail and told me that a bird was sitting right on my camera. I had been so absorbed with my painting that I had forgotten all about it. Soon after Jody left, I heard chickadees and pine grosbeaks at the feeder; I looked out and was very pleased to see birds all around the camera.

I thought my troubles were over; but they were not. The instant I started film going the birds still took off. The camera must have sounded like a lumber truck going by to their sensitive ears. The only way I would ever get movies close up would be to get the birds used to the noise.

With no film in the camera I waited at the feeder. Soon a chickadee came looping over and when he was about ten feet from me, I pressed the starter. The chickadee kept coming and settled on the fir tree. I wound up the camera and kept it running. I did this every time I heard birds coming, and after a few hours the chickadees and grosbeaks got used to the noise and I got my first movies at close range.

This operation had to be repeated for every specie of bird I wished to photograph, but if other birds who were used to the camera were at the feeder, the newcomers lost their fear quickly. The most difficult of all were the catbirds and robins. Their sense of hearing is much more keen than that of the seed-eaters, and the robin more so than the catbird. I made movies of several catbirds on my hand, but robins, although they would not hesitate to take raisins from my hand, would not allow the camera to be running any nearer than about six feet. They would take food placed within an inch of the camera, but I never found one who would stand the sound long enough for me to get movies.

Sometimes camera fans visit me who are not bird-wise but are very anxious to get bird pictures. Some of these visitors are wonderful photographers and take beautiful slides and pictures through the window of the kitchen door. The woodpecker's log feeder is near the window, and the photographer has a choice of ranges from about two to five feet. Many fine pictures of hairy woodpeckers,

**134**

downy woodpeckers, and chickadees have been taken on movie film; and slides and snapshots of all sizes, with many kinds of cameras. Pictures of the seed-eating birds on the feeding platform and on the branches of the fir tree are taken at ranges of about two to eight feet for the fir tree and about three to six feet for the feeder.

For outdoor pictures, the visitor may take a chair out and set up a tripod, and if he has the patience and makes no quick, sudden moves, he can get good pictures at the distance he wishes.

Once in a great while, a visitor with a lot of bird know-how is able to get pictures of a bird on his hand. I have to be very careful with this, because a wrong move could frighten the bird so much that it would leave and never come back, thus ruining endless hours of tedious work.

Three years back, in the early summer, I had five hand-tamed ruby-throated humming birds coming to my cups. These birds were very tame and would come to the hand of a total stranger. One day a bird-ignorant person had the idea he was going to get THE hummingbird film of all times. He followed the birds around from feeder cup to wild flower, even crawling up on them. The birds always have their eyes peeled for creeping predators and naturally thought the man with the camera wanted to make a meal out of them. He frightened them so much that they lost their trust of all humans; they left and never came back. There was not a single hummingbird on my place the rest of that year. I was away at the time, but I got the full story when I returned.

Before this happened, anyone was welcome to take pictures of my birds provided he followed my instructions to the letter; now I allow no one to do so unless he is known to

**135**

me to be a reliable bird man, and then only in my company and strictly under my supervision.

In 1957, I bought my first movie camera, a Brownie made by Kodak. My very first film was one of the best I have ever taken. I knew nothing about the Brownie, or any other camera for that matter, but the directions called for exposure 8 for average sunshine, and that was simple enough with Kodachrome film.

My next film was run off on a cloudy-to-hazy-sun day and I had to guess at the proper exposure. Some of this film was very good, but most of it wound up in my wood stove.

As time passed, I learned to judge the light conditions pretty well, but after five years, I still have considerable poorly exposed film. This usually happens when I use the camera on a day of changing light conditions and forget to adjust the exposure.

You may have noticed that some of the illustrations in this book were poorly exposed, but you understand, of course, that taking pictures of wild creatures must be done *when and where* the occasion provides. Wild creatures cannot be set up in good sunlight, so you have to take your chances, unless you are using one of the new cameras with automatic exposure control.

Some of the wildlife photographs we see today are extremely beautiful works of art. Most of these pictures are taken with powerful telescope lenses, and blinds are used.

You probably have noticed that most of the pictures you see of nesting songbirds are taken after the branches and foliage have been cut away so that a good unobstructed photo can be obtained. In photographing most songbirds this is necessary, but I often wonder what

**136**

happens to the nesting birds afterward. Is the nest left exposed to the sun and any jay or hawk that comes along?

I could have taken a very valuable film of the incubation and raising of a family of indigo buntings, but I could not do so at the expense of the birds. I had tamed the female so that she would sit on my thumb while she took grubs from the palm of my hand and fed her babies. The nest was two feet from the ground but pretty well hidden by leaves. I tied back some of the branches so the sun could strike the nest, and the instant the sun rays hit the babies, they twisted their tiny bodies into knots. I immediately let the shielding branches back and was unable to get movies worth keeping on account of the insufficient light.

I believe I have a lot more fun taking pictures my way. I use no blinds. I get birds at a few feet, animals at a few yards — even foxes.

This, of course, like the hand-taming, takes a lot of patience and time. First you must locate the bird or animal you wish to film. If you are a woodsman this will not be too difficult; if you are not too well versed in nature you may have a friend who can help you, or perhaps your local game warden will give you a little time.

Although I use only the normal lens when taking closeups of birds, I always keep a two-power telephoto lens on my Brownie. I do this because it is a screw-in type of lens and can be unscrewed in a second or two, but it takes much longer to put it on when needed, and I might lose a short run of a wild creature, such as three or four jumps of a deer. I never carry the camera in a case but hold it in my right hand with my finger on the starter as I go through the woods, and I can sight in a wild creature as fast as I can with a rifle.

In taking pictures of wild beings, the most important thing is to keep motionless as soon as your subject is sighted.

Last summer I called three different foxes up to within eighteen or twenty feet of me by imitating the sound of a pair of mating field mice. I already knew where these foxes hunted mice, and had made several trips to learn what time each fox could be seen in his mousing field.

Most wild creatures have a time-pattern — a muskrat will be on a piece of anchored driftwood at 6 A.M. every morning; a ruffed grouse will come to the same apple tree at 5 P.M. daily; a mink will poke his nose out from under a brook-bridge at twelve noon, and a fox will sit on a rock pile at 9 A.M.* The pattern is followed day after day, with little variation in the time, but it will, of course, change with the seasons.

One of the foxes I mentioned came to a nearby field at 8:10 A.M. every day. I waited for a day of good light, and was comfortably waiting for him at 7:45 A.M.

With the camera on my lap I sat motionless, and rolled my eyes from left to right while my ears were tuned in to Nature's sounds, listening for the voices of the red squirrel, blue jay, and nuthatch who would see the fox before he came into the open field and would let all wild creatures within hearing know that he was coming.

I had been sitting motionless for about fifteen minutes when the first red squirrel barked from some pines about two hundred yards back into the woods. The squirrel's warning was immediately repeated by a nuthatch.

---

* The times of day given here are arbitrary examples. The actual time differed for each.

**138**

It would be a few minutes before the fox would be in the open field, so I stood up and stretched, and lit a cigarette, then sat down again.

Now the jays, nuthatches, and squirrels were all sending out their warnings, and in another minute or so the fox stepped out into the field. He was about three hundred yards away, but I knew he would come a lot closer because there were two rock piles no more than one hundred feet from me and he would be sure to climb them and watch for mice below him in the grass.

The fox started heading my way and I watched him closely. In a few seconds he climbed the first rock pile and sat looking around. I waited until he turned so that the back of his head faced me, then I quickly brought the camera to my eye and rested my elbows on my knees and waited. Two barn swallows went at the fox, but he did not even duck as they swooped at him, missing his head by an inch or so.

The fox started for the next rock pile, and this brought him within hearing of my call. I started imitating a pair of mice mating, and the fox came in fast for about sixty feet, then slowed down and came on in stalking form. He did not hesitate, but came right along until he heard the camera rolling off film. He stopped, looked at me for a split second, then headed back the way he had come as fast as he could go. The wind was on my back while I was getting pictures of this fox, but he was so interested in getting something to eat that he had not noticed my scent until he had stopped.

It is always best if you can have the wind in your face while photographing any wild creature; even some of the birds have very keen scent. But of course you cannot change the wind and must do the best you can with wild creatures as you find them.

As important as the human scent is, it takes second place to motion as a picture hazard. While that fox was in the field he would have seen one of my fingers move if he had been looking my way.

I have taken movies of deer with my scent blowing right into them, but as long as I did not move, they were not frightened.

A great many hunters sacrifice smoking while hunting ducks or deer. This is not at all necessary. If the wind was right for a deer to smell smoke, the deer would also smell the hunter. It is not the smoke that jumps the animals, but the movements of the hunter in smoking.

Even a bear may come in close to a human if there is no movement. A very good example of this took place last October.

One evening just before dusk, Ed Musson came in with a black bear, and he told me he killed it under an old apple tree on Herbert Hardy's wood lot. Ed said that according to the signs he figured two bears were working that section.

The following morning just before dawn I was right there with my camera. I noticed the light breeze was coming directly from the east, so went to the farther side from where the bear were evidently coming in. This spot had been an orchard before I was born, but was now grown up with trees, with a little open space here and there.

I sat on a flat rock about twelve feet long to wait for the bear. In a few minutes dawn peeked through the fir trees, and I was able to get a good look at the old apple tree the bears had been coming to. A large raccoon was up in it, eating apples. About twenty minutes later two does

**140**

came in. One of them ate half an apple; the other picked up an apple but dropped it again. The two deer then went back into the woods to feed on mushrooms.

A porcupine came around the rock to my right; he was grunting like a little pig. A little later two ruffed grouse were under the apple tree. I sat and watched them picking the seeds and chipping pieces of apple out.

Now the light was good; the sun came up and it felt good on my face and hands. From behind the left end of the rock I was sitting on, I heard more grunting. I had never heard a bear make such a small grunting noise and thought it was another porcupine coming. Suddenly a beautiful black and golden head popped into view. I was fully unprepared for this, because my scent was being carried in the direction the bear had just come from.

I sat there with my head facing directly ahead as I had been for the last half hour and watched the bear out of the corner of my left eye. His eyes were shifting from side to side very rapidly as he came forward. Now I could see all of him. He weighed about one hundred and fifty pounds, was in beautiful fur. He was still grunting, and now he turned and looked me in the face, and instantly I saw a flash of fear. I swung the camera at him as fast as I could, but he was so fast that I got only five or six frames with the camera about ten feet from him.

Maybe I pulled a boner on this one. Maybe if I had spoken softly to him and remained motionless, the bear might have gone to the apple tree.

For all close-ups of wild things I can get near to, I use the normal lens. The two-power telephoto lens will not, on my simple camera, give a passable picture if used any closer than eight feet, which gives you the equivalent detail of a picture taken with the normal lens at four feet.

Using the normal lens, I get passable pictures at two feet. By passable pictures, I do not mean fair pictures as photography is judged, but shots that are good enough to be enjoyed. As you can see by the position of the hand in some of the illustrations in this book, the only way they could have been taken was with the bird on one hand and the camera held to the eye with the other. This brings the bird a little less than two feet from the camera.

If the telescope two-power lens were used on a hummingbird, it would appear no larger than a house fly.

I have a film of hornets coming to and leaving their nest. This film was taken with the camera about a foot from the nest. Some of the insects are a little blurred as they fly within inches of the lens, but most of them show up remarkably well. I have also taken some nice pictures of butterflies in bright sun at about fifteen inches.

Do not feel discouraged if your first few attempts at hand-taming are failures, because this may happen to the best of naturalists. There is just as much individualism among all wild creatures as there is among people. It may be that not a single bird was tamable in the flock you worked with.

I have found that in some species most of the birds will in time take food from the hand. In another specie, there may be only three out of ten, and in some not more than one or two in a hundred.

The species you work on will, of course, be decided by the types of birds you have at your feeder. If you have red cardinals I cannot help you, because I have never had them. I have seen many of them; I know their notes and the kind of food they eat, but I have never hand-tamed one, so cannot give you any dependable information on the bird.

142

Here at Great Pond, Maine, most of the pine grosbeaks will hand-tame. About sixty per cent of the redpolls will take food from the hand. About fifty per cent of the chickadees and thirty per cent of the purple finches will hand-tame.

In every specie of bird there are several individuals who will tame more readily than others of the same specie; on the other hand, there are some that will never tame. (Some people enjoy certain types of food more than others. I enjoy a good meal myself, but not as much as some people do. On the other hand, I would do almost anything to bite into one of Geri Butler's lemon pies.) Every specie of bird has some kind of food he prefers above all other foods. The purple finch will kill himself on flax seed if he has the chance. The white-breasted nuthatch, the evening grosbeak, pine grosbeak and chickadee prefer sunflower seed. The goldfinch likes thistle. The red-breasted nuthatch, the downy and hairy woodpeckers, like suet. The robin and catbird are very fond of raisins and cooking currants. If you cannot entice any one of the above birds to your hand with the food mentioned, you can be fairly certain that it is impossible to tame that individual.

A friend once asked me if it would not be easier and save time to trap the birds and tame them in a cage, as I did while collecting birds for the pet market, and then liberate them.

This would be impossible because an adult wild bird who has been caged immediately becomes a wild bird again as soon as he is free.

When a healthy bird is trapped and confined he can be coaxed to take food from the hand and he can lose his fear of man, but he still does not like being confined in a cage and will always remember that although he is no

**143**

longer afraid, he has been abused. Once he can fly in his natural habitat he will make sure it will not happen again if he can help it. He will not come near your hand and will warn every bird in his flock to keep away from you. He may go into the trap-cage again for something to eat, but not if he sees you around. Wild creatures do not like to be handled, and once a hand closes on a bird he never forgets it.

Wild birds are extremely clever in figuring things out. They seem to know when they are being helped. Proof of this is plainly seen when you pick up a helpless, crippled bird. This is the only time it does not greatly resent being confined. I have handled dozens of crippled birds, and in every case where it has recovered, even if it has been confined only a few days, the bird will come to the hand after it has its liberty. This is proof enough that the crippled bird knows and appreciates that you are helping it. It is the handling of healthy birds that have been banded that makes them impossible to hand-tame, and if you *are* successful in hand-taming one of these, you can feel pretty sure that it had been injured at some time and had the right treatment while in captivity.

Birds taken from the nest as babies and raised in a cage would come to the hand when released, but that would be like catching trout with a net. You would not be hand-taming a wild bird. It merely would be coming to feed like a barnyard chicken.

Now as I wind this up, I can hear the children — all six of them — getting out of our tiny schoolhouse. It is lunch time, and I think I will slap a tender venison steak in my battered old fry-pan and leave you to enjoy your birds.

**144**